MW01027154

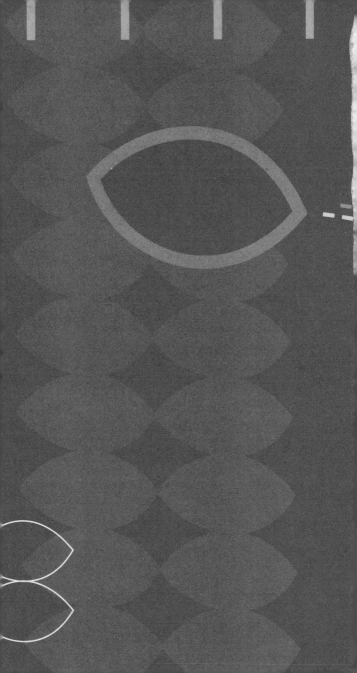

To:

....

Run in such a way
as to get the prize ...
a crown that will last forever.
1 Corinthians 9:24-25

From:

....

Touchdown! God's Words of Life
from the NIV Sports Devotional Bible
Copyright © 2004 by The Zondervan Corporation
ISBN 0-310-80599-6

The devotionals in this gift book were taken from the
Sports Devotional Bible, New International Version,
Dave Branon, General Editor

Requests for information should be addressed to:
Inspirio, the gift group of Zondervan
Grand Rapids, Michigan 49530
http://www.inspiriogifts.com

Associate Publisher: Tom Dean
Compiler: Robin Schmitt
Design Manager: Val Buick
Designer: Amy Peterman/Peterman Design

Printed in China
04 05 06/ HK/ 5 4 3 2 1

TOUCH DOWN!

God's Words of Life from
the NIV Sports Devotional Bible

inspirio™

GOD'S WORDS OF LIFE ON

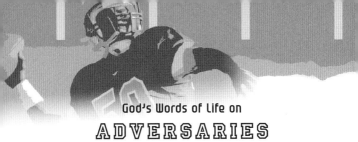

Jesus said, "Love your enemies, do good to those who hate you, bless those who curse you, pray for those who mistreat you. If someone strikes you on one cheek, turn to him the other also. If someone takes your cloak, do not stop him from taking your tunic. Give to everyone who asks you, and if anyone takes what belongs to you, do not demand it back. Do to others as you would have them do to you. If you love those who love you, what credit is that to you? Even 'sinners' love those who love them. And if you do good to those who are good to you, what credit is that to you? Even 'sinners' do that. And if you lend to those from whom you expect repayment, what credit is that to you? Even 'sinners' lend to 'sinners,' expecting to be repaid in full. But love your enemies, do good to them, and lend to them without expecting to get anything back. Then your reward will be great, and you will be sons of the Most High, because he is kind to the ungrateful and wicked. Be merciful, just as your Father is merciful."

Luke 6:27–36

Forgive us our sins,
  for we also forgive everyone who sins against us.

Luke 11:4

Do not repay anyone evil for evil.

Romans 12:17

ADVERSARIES

....

Jesus said, "If your brother sins, rebuke him, and if he repents, forgive him. If he sins against you seven times in a day, and seven times comes back to you and says, 'I repent,' forgive him."

Luke 17:3–4

Jesus said, "The kingdom of heaven is like a king who wanted to settle accounts with his servants. As he began the settlement, a man who owed him ten thousand talents was brought to him. Since he was not able to pay, the master ordered that he and his wife and his children and all that he had be sold to repay the debt. The servant fell on his knees before him. 'Be patient with me,' he begged, 'and I will pay back everything.' The servant's master took pity on him, canceled the debt and let him go. But when that servant went out, he found one of his fellow servants who owed him a hundred denarii. He grabbed him and began to choke him. 'Pay back what you owe me!' he demanded. His fellow servant fell to his knees and begged him, 'Be patient with me, and I will pay you back.' But he refused. Instead, he went off and had the man thrown into prison until he could pay the debt. When the other servants saw what had happened, they were greatly distressed and went and told their master every-thing that had happened. Then the master called the servant in. 'You wicked servant,' he said, 'I canceled all that debt of yours because you begged me to. Shouldn't you have had mercy on your fellow servant just as I had on you?' In anger his master turned him over to the jail-ers to be tortured until he should pay back all he owed. This is how my heavenly Father will treat each of you unless you forgive your brother from your heart."

Matthew 18:23–35

God's Words of Life on

ADVERSARIES

Jesus said, "When you stand praying, if you hold any-thing against anyone, forgive him, so that your Father in heaven may forgive you your sins."

Mark 11:25

"Do not seek revenge or bear a grudge against one of your people, but love your neighbor as yourself. I am the LORD."

Leviticus 19:18

If your enemy is hungry, give him food to eat;
  if he is thirsty, give him water to drink.
In doing this, you will heap burning coals on his head,
  and the LORD will reward you.

Proverbs 25:21–22

If anyone has caused grief, he has not so much grieved me as he has grieved all of you, to some extent—not to put it too severely. The punishment inflicted on him by the majority is sufficient for him. Now instead, you ought to forgive and comfort him, so that he will not be over-whelmed by excessive sorrow. I urge you, therefore, to reaffirm your love for him. The reason I wrote you was to see if you would stand the test and be obedient in everything. If you forgive anyone, I also forgive him. And what I have forgiven—if there was anything to forgive—I have forgiven in the sight of Christ for your sake, in order that Satan might not outwit us. For we are not unaware of his schemes.

2 Corinthians 2:5–11

God's Words of Life on
ADVERSARIES

....

Jesus said, "If you forgive men when they sin against you, your heavenly Father will also forgive you. But if you do not forgive men their sins, your Father will not forgive your sins."

Matthew 6:14–15

Jesus said, "You have heard that it was said, 'Love your neighbor and hate your enemy.' But I tell you: Love your enemies and pray for those who persecute you, that you may be sons of your Father in heaven. He causes his sun to rise on the evil and the good, and sends rain on the righteous and the unrighteous. If you love those who love you, what reward will you get? Are not even the tax collectors doing that? And if you greet only your brothers, what are you doing more than others? Do not even [unbelievers] do that? Be perfect, therefore, as your heavenly Father is perfect."

Matthew 5:43–48

As God's chosen people, holy and dearly loved, clothe yourselves with compassion, kindness, humility, gentleness and patience. Bear with each other and forgive whatever grievances you may have against one another. Forgive as the Lord forgave you. And over all these virtues put on love, which binds them all together in perfect unity.

Colossians 3:12–14

Do not be overcome by evil, but overcome evil with good.

Romans 12:21

God's Words of Life on

ADVERSARIES

Jesus said, "Do not judge, and you will not be judged. Do not condemn, and you will not be condemned. Forgive, and you will be forgiven."

Luke 6:37

Jesus said, "As you are going with your adversary to the magistrate, try hard to be reconciled to him on the way."

Luke 12:58

Get rid of all bitterness, rage and anger, brawling and slander, along with every form of malice. Be kind and compassionate to one another, forgiving each other, just as in Christ God forgave you.

Ephesians 4:31–32

Once you were alienated from God and were enemies in your minds because of your evil behavior. But now he has reconciled you by Christ's physical body through death to present you holy in his sight, without blemish and free from accusation.

Colossians 1:21–22

Jonah was greatly displeased and became angry. He prayed to the LORD, "O LORD, is this not what I said when I was still at home? That is why I was so quick to flee to Tarshish. I knew that you are a gracious and compassionate God, slow to anger and abounding in love, a God who relents from sending calamity."

Jonah 4:1–2

ADVERSARIES

Jonah wanted to go for the kill.

When he finally got to Nineveh to proclaim God's message to the people, he decided that the best thing for God to do was to wipe the city out. Maybe it was a pride thing. After all, once you've told a bunch of people they're going to die, you'll look pretty silly if they don't get so much as a scratch.

So when he found out that Nineveh would be forgiven (Jonah 4), he was ticked. Really ticked.

Jonah was like a good defensive unit in football. Once they get momentum on their side and realize they have a chance to win, they go for the kill. They tackle with ferocity and hunt down the quarterback like a lion going after a baby gazelle.

Jonah wanted to blitz Nineveh.

But he forgot about God's compassion. He forgot that God would rather bless the world than condemn it. He forgot that God wants the sacrifice of repentance more than anything else.

Jonah had his sights set on revenge and judgment. God chose mercy.

Does Jonah sound like anyone we know?

God has a better way to treat enemies than we do. Let's learn from Jonah's mistake.

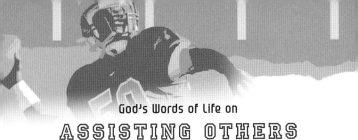

God's Words of Life on

ASSISTING OTHERS

Jesus said, "Come, you who are blessed by my Father; take your inheritance, the kingdom prepared for you since the creation of the world. For I was hungry and you gave me something to eat, I was thirsty and you gave me something to drink, I was a stranger and you invited me in, I needed clothes and you clothed me, I was sick and you looked after me, I was in prison and you came to visit me."

Matthew 25:34–36

"He did what was right and just,
    so all went well with him.
He defended the cause of the poor and needy,
    and so all went well.
Is that not what it means to know me?"
    declares the LORD.

Jeremiah 22:15–16

Last year you were the first not only to give but also to have the desire to do so. Now finish the work, so that your eager willingness to do it may be matched by your completion of it, according to your means. For if the willingness is there, the gift is acceptable according to what one has, not according to what he does not have.

2 Corinthians 8:10–12

A wife of noble character ... opens her arms to the poor
    and extends her hands to the needy.

Proverbs 31:10, 20

God's Words of Life on
ASSISTING OTHERS

If one of your countrymen becomes poor and is unable to support himself among you, help him ... so he can continue to live among you. Do not take interest of any kind from him, but fear your God, so that your country-man may continue to live among you. You must not lend him money at interest or sell him food at a profit.

Leviticus 25:35–37

All the believers were one in heart and mind. No one claimed that any of his possessions was his own, but they shared everything they had.... There were no needy persons among them. For from time to time those who owned lands or houses sold them, brought the money from the sales and put it at the apostles' feet, and it was distributed to anyone as he had need.

Acts 4:32, 34–35

Religion that God our Father accepts as pure and faultless is this: to look after orphans and widows in their distress and to keep oneself from being polluted by the world.

James 1:27

He who has been stealing must steal no longer, but must work, doing something useful with his own hands, that he may have something to share with those in need.

Ephesians 4:28

God's Words of Life on

ASSISTING OTHERS

He who is kind to the poor lends to the LORD,
   and he will reward him for what he has done.

Proverbs 19:17

Do not withhold good from those who deserve it,
   when it is in your power to act.

Proverbs 3:27

*If there is a poor man among your brothers in any of the
towns of the land that the LORD your God is giving you,
do not be hardhearted or tightfisted toward your poor
brother. Rather be openhanded and freely lend him
whatever he needs.*

Deuteronomy 15:7–8

We should continue to remember the poor.

Galatians 2:10

*In Joppa there was a disciple named Tabitha ... who was
always doing good and helping the poor.*

Acts 9:36

*Give proper recognition to those widows who are really
in need.*

1 Timothy 5:3

*If a man's gift is ... contributing to the needs of others,
let him give generously.*

Romans 12:6, 8

ASSISTING OTHERS

Jesus said, "When you give a luncheon or dinner, do not invite your friends, your brothers or relatives, or your rich neighbors; if you do, they may invite you back and so you will be repaid. But when you give a banquet, invite the poor, the crippled, the lame, the blind, and you will be blessed. Although they cannot repay you, you will be repaid at the resurrection of the righteous."

Luke 14:12–14

I rescued the poor who cried for help,
  and the fatherless who had none to assist him.
The man who was dying blessed me;
  I made the widow's heart sing.
I put on righteousness as my clothing;
  justice was my robe and my turban.
I was eyes to the blind
  and feet to the lame.
I was a father to the needy;
  I took up the case of the stranger.

Job 29:12–16

God has heard your prayer and remembered your gifts to the poor.

Acts 10:31

God is not unjust; he will not forget your work and the love you have shown him as you have helped his people and continue to help them.

Hebrews 6:10

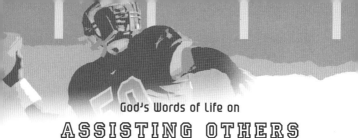

God's Words of Life on

ASSISTING OTHERS

....

Jesus said, "Give, and it will be given to you. A good measure, pressed down, shaken together and running over, will be poured into your lap. For with the measure you use, it will be measured to you."

Luke 6:38

There will always be poor people in the land. Therefore I command you to be openhanded toward your brothers and toward the poor and needy in your land.

Deuteronomy 15:11

Jesus said, "The Spirit of the Lord is on me,
    because he has anointed me
    to preach good news to the poor.
He has sent me to proclaim freedom for the prisoners
    and recovery of sight for the blind,
to release the oppressed,
    to proclaim the year of the Lord's favor."

Luke 4:18–19

Jesus said, "When you give to the needy, do not announce it with trumpets, as the hypocrites do in the synagogues and on the streets, to be honored by men. I tell you the truth, they have received their reward in full. But when you give to the needy, do not let your left hand know what your right hand is doing, so that your giving may be in secret. Then your Father, who sees what is done in secret, will reward you."

Matthew 6:2–4

Devotional Thought on

ASSISTING OTHERS

Reggie White was a defensive end who retired as the NFL's all-time sack champion. But he played almost his entire career without going to the Super Bowl. Only in his last two seasons with the Green Bay Packers did he get to play in football's top contest.

He once told ESPN's Andrea Kramer: "As a football player, it's the ultimate goal. It's what I've worked for; it's what I've sweated for. That's why I keep myself prepared." But then he said something else that we can all relate to. Reggie said, "What if I do win the championship, put a nice ring on my finger, but never did anything to impact anybody's life? Or what if I didn't win the Super Bowl but had an impact on millions? That's the greatest Super Bowl I could ever be a part of. I would rather win the Super Bowl as a human being."

Of course, Reggie did win football's Super Bowl in 1997.

But he also wins life's Super Bowl. In many ways, Reggie has reached out to help people—poor people, discouraged people, people who need to know about Jesus Christ.

God doesn't expect us all to be champion athletes, but he is honored and glorified when we help the people he has created. It's our way of winning life's Super Bowl.

Jesus said, "There was a man who had two sons. The younger one said to his father, 'Father, give me my share of the estate.' So he divided his property between them. Not long after that, the younger son got together all he had, set off for a distant country and there squandered his wealth in wild living. After he had spent everything, there was a severe famine in that whole country, and he began to be in need. So he went and hired himself out to a citizen of that country, who sent him to his fields to feed pigs. He longed to fill his stomach with the pods that the pigs were eating, but no one gave him anything. When he came to his senses, he said, 'How many of my father's hired men have food to spare, and here I am starving to death! I will set out and go back to my father and say to him: Father, I have sinned against heaven and against you. I am no longer worthy to be called your son; make me like one of your hired men.' So he got up and went to his father. But while he was still a long way off, his father saw him and was filled with compassion for him; he ran to his son, threw his arms around him and kissed him. The son said to him, 'Father, I have sinned against heaven and against you. I am no longer worthy to be called your son.' But the father said to his servants, 'Quick! Bring the best robe and put it on him. Put a ring on his finger and sandals on his feet. Bring the fattened calf and kill it. Let's have a feast and celebrate. For this son of mine was dead and is alive again; he was lost and is found.' So they began to celebrate."

Luke 15:11–24

God's Words of Life on
COMEBACKS

Return to the LORD, the God of Abraham, Isaac and Israel, that he may return to you.... The LORD your God is gracious and compassionate. He will not turn his face from you if you return to him.

2 Chronicles 30:6, 9

If you return to the Almighty, you will be restored.

Job 22:23

If from there you seek the LORD your God, you will find him if you look for him with all your heart and with all your soul. When you are in distress and all these things have happened to you, then in later days you will return to the LORD your God and obey him. For the LORD your God is a merciful God; he will not abandon or destroy you or forget the covenant with your forefathers, which he confirmed to them by oath.

Deuteronomy 4:29–31

"I have swept away your offenses like a cloud,
     your sins like the morning mist.
Return to me,
     for I have redeemed you,"
          declares the LORD.

Isaiah 44:22

The ransomed of the LORD will return.
     They will enter Zion with singing;
     everlasting joy will crown their heads.
Gladness and joy will overtake them,
     and sorrow and sighing will flee away.

Isaiah 51:11

God's Words of Life on
COMEBACKS

....

When you and your children return to the LORD your God and obey him with all your heart and with all your soul according to everything I command you today, then the LORD your God will restore your fortunes and have compassion on you.

Deuteronomy 30:2–3

Return to him you have so greatly revolted against.

Isaiah 31:6

"If you repent, I will restore you
   that you may serve me,"
     declares the LORD.

Jeremiah 15:19

Let us examine our ways and test them,
   and let us return to the LORD.

Lamentations 3:40

Take words with you
   and return to the LORD.
Say to him:
   "Forgive all our sins
and receive us graciously."

Hosea 14:2

God's Words of Life on
COMEBACKS

Repent, for the kingdom of heaven is near.

Matthew 3:2

Jesus said, "You have forsaken your first love. Remember the height from which you have fallen! Repent and do the things you did at first."

Revelation 2:4–5

Rend your heart
  and not your garments.
Return to the LORD your God,
  for he is gracious and compassionate,
slow to anger and abounding in love,
  and he relents from sending calamity.

Joel 2:13

Repent and be baptized, every one of you, in the name of Jesus Christ for the forgiveness of your sins. And you will receive the gift of the Holy Spirit. The promise is for you and your children and for all who are far off—for all whom the Lord our God will call.

Acts 2:38–39

My brothers, if one of you should wander from the truth and someone should bring him back, remember this: Whoever turns a sinner from the error of his way will save him from death and cover over a multitude of sins.

James 5:19–20

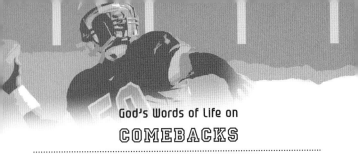

God's Words of Life on
COMEBACKS

....

Come back to your senses as you ought, and stop sinning.
1 Corinthians 15:34

Repent, then, and turn to God, so that your sins may be wiped out, that times of refreshing may come from the Lord.

Acts 3:19

"Come out from them
    and be separate,
        says the Lord.
Touch no unclean thing,
    and I will receive you."
"I will be a Father to you,
    and you will be my sons and daughters,
        says the Lord Almighty."

2 Corinthians 6:17–18

"The time has come," Jesus said. "The kingdom of God is near. Repent and believe the good news!"

Mark 1:15

"I will give them a heart to know me, that I am the LORD. They will be my people, and I will be their God, for they will return to me with all their heart."

Jeremiah 24:7

Devotional Thought on

COMEBACKS

Bill Curry was a longtime college football coach for such schools as the University of Kentucky and the University of Alabama. During his years as a head coach, he maintained a strong testimony of faith in Christ.

He didn't always have that spiritual sensitivity, however. For a while during his younger days, he drifted from the faith and went out on his own, seeking the world's wares.

Here's part of his story of those lost years:

> With my ego and my personality, I thought it was necessary to gravitate in the wrong direction, but the incredible thing about Christ is that he is still there. He's always there and he's always waiting.
>
> When those of us who become prodigal sons decide to come back, he is excited to see us. I came back, and that was sort of a dramatic turn of events in my life. The omnipresence of Christ in the world, for anybody who will watch and listen and open up to him, is the most remarkable thing.

Just like the father in the story of the lost son in Luke 15, Jesus awaits our return. When we stray from the path of righteousness that is so clearly set out for us in Scripture, he eagerly woos us and longs for us to return to him.

He's waiting. Do you need to run into his open arms?

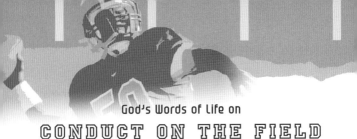

God's Words of Life on

CONDUCT ON THE FIELD

Jesus said, "You are the light of the world. A city on a hill cannot be hidden. Neither do people light a lamp and put it under a bowl. Instead they put it on its stand, and it gives light to everyone in the house. In the same way, let your light shine before men, that they may see your good deeds and praise your Father in heaven."

Matthew 5:14–16

"I am God Almighty; walk before me and be blameless."

Genesis 17:1

The noble man makes noble plans,
    and by noble deeds he stands.

Isaiah 32:8

I will sing of your love and justice;
    to you, O LORD, I will sing praise.
I will be careful to lead a blameless life—
    when will you come to me?
I will walk in my house
    with blameless heart.
I will set before my eyes
    no vile thing.

Psalm 101:1–3

CONDUCT ON THE FIELD

"I the LORD search the heart
   and examine the mind,
to reward a man according to his conduct,
   according to what his deeds deserve."

Jeremiah 17:10

*Be careful to do what the LORD your God has commanded
you; do not turn aside to the right or to the left. Walk in all
the way that the LORD your God has commanded you, so
that you may live and prosper.*

Deuteronomy 5:32–33

He whose walk is blameless is kept safe.

Proverbs 28:18

*We know that we have come to know God if we obey
his commands. The man who says, "I know him," but
does not do what he commands is a liar, and the truth is
not in him. But if anyone obeys his word, God's love is
truly made complete in him. This is how we know we
are in him: Whoever claims to live in him must walk as
Jesus did.*

1 John 2:3–6

Stand at the crossroads and look;
   ask for the ancient paths,
ask where the good way is, and walk in it,
   and you will find rest for your souls.

Jeremiah 6:16

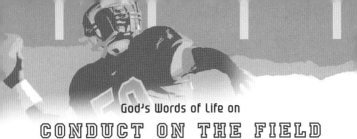

God's Words of Life on

CONDUCT ON THE FIELD

The LORD God is a sun and shield;
    the LORD bestows favor and honor;
no good thing does he withhold
    from those whose walk is blameless.

Psalm 84:11

*O great and powerful God, whose name is the LORD
Almighty, great are your purposes and mighty are your
deeds. Your eyes are open to all the ways of men; you
reward everyone according to his conduct and as his
deeds deserve.*

Jeremiah 32:18–19

Let us walk in the light of the LORD.

Isaiah 2:5

"Can anyone hide in secret places
    so that I cannot see him?"
        declares the LORD.
"Do not I fill heaven and earth?"
        declares the LORD.

Jeremiah 23:24

*The night is nearly over; the day is almost here. So let us
put aside the deeds of darkness and put on the armor of
light. Let us behave decently, as in the daytime.*

Romans 13:12–13

Devotional Thought on
CONDUCT ON THE FIELD

Professional athletes run, but they can't hide.

The unblinking eye of the ubiquitous TV camera records every move they make, turning their great plays into highlight film fodder and their errors into blooper reel candidates. And though a bit bothersome to the trouble-makers in sports, it also makes their violations available for league officials to review.

That's why in the NFL, for instance, a player might plant a dirty hit on a player on Sunday and not even draw a flag. But when league officials review the tapes later in the week, they may request a donation of $25,000 to the "I made a big mistake" fund.

God has always had his eye on the situations going on in our lives. He has always kept a record of what has been going on in our day-to-day existence. "Nothing in all creation is hidden from God's sight" (Hebrews 4:13).

So, what does this mean—this record-keeping? It means that someday we will have to give an account for the way we have lived.

It's a sobering thought, isn't it? A thought that should spur us to godly living and to loving care for others. Because nothing is hidden, we must "hold firmly to the faith we profess" (Hebrews 4:14) and lean heavily on Jesus, our high priest, to make us the people he wants us to be.

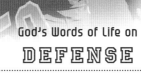

God's Words of Life on
DEFENSE

Jesus was led by the Spirit into the desert to be tempted by the devil. After fasting forty days and forty nights, he was hungry. The tempter came to him and said, "If you are the Son of God, tell these stones to become bread." Jesus answered, "It is written: 'Man does not live on bread alone, but on every word that comes from the mouth of God.'"

Matthew 4:1–4

Jesus said, "Pray so that you will not fall into temptation."
Luke 22:46

Jesus said, "Simon, Simon, Satan has asked to sift you as wheat. But I have prayed for you, Simon, that your faith may not fail."
Luke 22:31-32

Look to the LORD and his strength.
1 Chronicles 16:11

The God of Israel gives power and strength to his people.
Psalm 68:35

My flesh and my heart may fail,
but God is the strength of my heart
and my portion forever.

Psalm 73:26

God's Words of Life on
DEFENSE

Since we have a great high priest who has gone through the heavens, Jesus the Son of God, let us hold firmly to the faith we profess. For we do not have a high priest who is unable to sympathize with our weaknesses, but we have one who has been tempted in every way, just as we are—yet was without sin.

Hebrews 4:14–15

O LORD, be not far off;
O my Strength, come quickly to help me.

Psalm 22:19

Do not set foot on the path of the wicked
or walk in the way of evil men.
Avoid it, do not travel on it;
turn from it and go on your way.

Proverbs 4:14–15

You are my hiding place, O LORD;
you will protect me from trouble
and surround me with songs of deliverance.

Psalm 32:7

O LORD, be our strength every morning,
our salvation in time of distress.

Isaiah 33:2

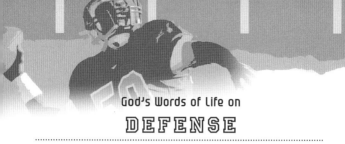

God's Words of Life on

DEFENSE

Because Jesus himself suffered when he was tempted, he is able to help those who are being tempted.

Hebrews 2:18

O Lord, you armed me with strength for battle;
    you made my adversaries bow at my feet.
You made my enemies turn their backs in flight,
    and I destroyed my foes.

2 Samuel 22:40

God has the power to help.

2 Chronicles 25:8

Is any one of you in trouble? He should pray.

James 5:13

The Lord saves his anointed;
    he answers him from his holy heaven
    with the saving power of his right hand.

Psalm 20:6

The Lord will guard the feet of his saints.

1 Samuel 2:9

God anointed Jesus of Nazareth with the Holy Spirit and power, and ... he went around doing good and healing all who were under the power of the devil, because God was with him.

Acts 10:38

God's Words of Life on
DEFENSE

....

Be strong in the Lord and in his mighty power. Put on the full armor of God so that you can take your stand against the devil's schemes. For our struggle is not against flesh and blood, but against the rulers, against the authorities, against the powers of this dark world and against the spiritual forces of evil in the heavenly realms.

Ephesians 6:10–12

With us is the LORD our God to help us and to fight our battles.

2 Chronicles 32:8

In the LORD I take refuge.

Psalm 11:1

"Not by might nor by power, but by my Spirit," says the LORD Almighty.

Zechariah 4:6

David found strength in the LORD his God.

1 Samuel 30:6

The Lord is faithful, and he will strengthen and protect you from the evil one.

2 Thessalonians 3:3

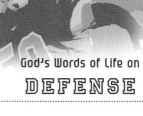

God's Words of Life on
DEFENSE

Put on the full armor of God, so that when the day of evil comes, you may be able to stand your ground, and after you have done everything, to stand. Stand firm then, with the belt of truth buckled around your waist, with the breastplate of righteousness in place, and with your feet fitted with the readiness that comes from the gospel of peace. In addition to all this, take up the shield of faith, with which you can extinguish all the flaming arrows of the evil one. Take the helmet of salvation and the sword of the Spirit, which is the word of God.

Ephesians 6:13–17

Test everything. Hold on to the good. Avoid every kind of evil.

1 Thessalonians 5:21–22

Build yourselves up in your most holy faith and pray in the Holy Spirit. Keep yourselves in God's love as you wait for the mercy of our Lord Jesus Christ to bring you to eternal life.

Jude 20–21

You ... through faith are shielded by God's power.

1 Peter 1:4–5

As servants of God we commend ourselves in every way: in great endurance; in troubles, hardships and distresses; ... in truthful speech and in the power of God; with weapons of righteousness in the right hand and in the left.

2 Corinthians 6:4, 7

Devotional Thought on
DEFENSE

Life in the NFL.

"It's a fast lifestyle for those who aren't Christians. The things that you see in everyday life are accelerated at an unbelievable level."

Brent Jones, who played for many years with the San Francisco 49ers, knows how important it is for Christian athletes to overcome the unavoidable temptations that plague those who live lives as pro athletes.

Our battles may not be the same as those of sports stars, but our temptations are just as much a part of our lives.

That's why Jesus' example of how to beat temptation (illustrated in Matthew 4:1–11) should be our guide. Let's look at Jesus' strategy.

First, Jesus quoted Scripture. He leaned on the truths of God's Word to direct his thinking. The more Scripture we tuck away in our hearts, the better we can battle Satan.

Second, Jesus made sure he remained in God's will. Satan attempted to test God, but Jesus made it clear that it was God's will he was following, not his own or someone else's.

Third, Jesus demonstrated that we should put nothing before God. When we give in to temptation, we are elevating something else to a place above God and his righteous commands.

Are you facing temptation? Do what Jesus did. Fight temptation off with the Word and with a total trust in God.

God's Words of Life on

DOMINATION

Do nothing out of selfish ambition or vain conceit, but in humility consider others better than yourselves. Each of you should look not only to your own interests, but also to the interests of others.

Philippians 2:3–4

[Jesus told his disciples], "You know that the rulers of the Gentiles lord it over them, and their high officials exercise authority over them. Not so with you. Instead, whoever wants to become great among you must be your servant, and whoever wants to be first must be your slave—just as the Son of Man did not come to be served, but to serve, and to give his life as a ransom for many."

Matthew 20:25–28

If you harbor bitter envy and selfish ambition in your hearts, do not boast about it or deny the truth. Such "wisdom" does not come down from heaven but is earthly, unspiritual, of the devil. For where you have envy and selfish ambition, there you find disorder and every evil practice. But the wisdom that comes from heaven is first of all pure; then peace-loving, considerate, submissive, full of mercy and good fruit, impartial and sincere.

James 3:14–17

God's Words of Life on

DOMINATION

The acts of the sinful nature are obvious: ... hatred, discord, jealousy, fits of rage, selfish ambition.... I warn you, as I did before, that those who live like this will not inherit the kingdom of God. But the fruit of the Spirit is love, joy, peace, patience, kindness, goodness, faithfulness, gentleness and self-control.

Galatians 5:19–23

Jesus said, "The last will be first, and the first will be last."

Matthew 20:16

To the elders among you, I appeal as a fellow elder, a witness of Christ's sufferings and one who also will share in the glory to be revealed: Be shepherds of God's flock that is under your care, serving as overseers—not because you must, but because you are willing, as God wants you to be; not greedy for money, but eager to serve; not lording it over those entrusted to you, but being examples to the flock. And when the Chief Shepherd appears, you will receive the crown of glory that will never fade away.

1 Peter 5:1–4

God's Words of Life on

DOMINATION

It was just before the Passover Feast. Jesus knew that the time had come for him to leave this world and go to the Father. Having loved his own who were in the world, he now showed them the full extent of his love.... Jesus knew that the Father had put all things under his power, and that he had come from God and was returning to God; so he got up from the meal, took off his outer clothing, and wrapped a towel around his waist. After that, he poured water into a basin and began to wash his disciples' feet, drying them with the towel that was wrapped around him.

John 13:1, 3–5

Christ Jesus, being in very nature God,
   did not consider equality with God something to
     be grasped,
but made himself nothing,
   taking the very nature of a servant.

Philippians 2:6–7

Jesus said, "A new command I give you: Love one another. As I have loved you, so you must love one another. By this all men will know that you are my disciples, if you love one another."

John 13:34–35

Husbands, love your wives, just as Christ loved the church and gave himself up for her.

Ephesians 5:25

Devotional Thought on

DOMINATION

....

Football players are nothing if not dominators. An offensive lineman must dominate his opponent or his opponent will soon be turning the quarterback into a crumpled heap.

One of those dominators was Ken Ruettgers, who protected Brett Favre and a host of other signal-callers for the Green Bay Packers for 12 years. In 1987 Ruettgers was voted the Packers' Offensive Player of the Year. There's no question that Ken Ruettgers could dominate— on the football field, that is.

But when he got home to his wife, Sheryl, he realized that his time to dominate was over. When Ken got home, the playbook called for something far different. It called for love.

So how does a football player who earns his living by pushing people around demonstrate love instead of dominance to his wife? Ken suggested that we can all do that "by serving her and by giving up our lives for our wives, as Christ did for the church. It's not always easy to do that, especially when we're blitzed with all kinds of other messages about wanting to fulfill our dreams and getting what we deserve. It's tough."

Just as Jesus Christ completely gave himself up to provide salvation for the church, a husband is also to completely give himself up for his wife's good. When that happens, the husband will earn the respect of his wife.

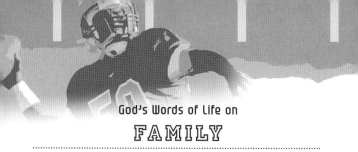

God's Words of Life on

FAMILY

Blessed are all who fear the LORD,
    who walk in his ways.
You will eat the fruit of your labor;
    blessings and prosperity will be yours.
Your wife will be like a fruitful vine
    within your house;
your sons will be like olive shoots
    around your table.
Thus is the man blessed
    who fears the LORD.

Psalm 128:1–4

As for me and my household, we will serve the LORD.

Joshua 24:15

*The LORD said, "I have chosen Abraham, so that he will
direct his children and his household after him to keep
the way of the LORD by doing what is right and just, so
that the LORD will bring about for Abraham what he has
promised him."*

Genesis 18:19

*He must manage his own family well and see that his
children obey him with proper respect.*

1 Timothy 3:4

God's Words of Life on
FAMILY

Sons are a heritage from the LORD,
  children a reward from him.
Like arrows in the hands of a warrior
  are sons born in one's youth.
Blessed is the man
  whose quiver is full of them.

Psalm 127:3–5

The house of the righteous contains great treasure.
Proverbs 15:6

Unless the LORD builds the house,
  its builders labor in vain.

Psalm 127:1

*Every house is built by someone, but God is the builder
of everything.*

Hebrews 3:4

*He was filled with joy because he had come to believe
in God—he and his whole family.*

Acts 16:34

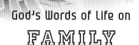

God's Words of Life on
FAMILY

....

Jesus said, "Go home to your family and tell them how much the Lord has done for you."

Mark 5:19

David returned home to bless his family.

1 Chronicles 16:43

At Caesarea there was a man named Cornelius, a centurion in what was known as the Italian Regiment. He and all his family were devout and God-fearing; he gave generously to those in need and prayed to God regularly.

Acts 10:1–2

By faith Noah, when warned about things not yet seen, in holy fear built an ark to save his family.

Hebrews 11:7

The LORD blesses the home of the righteous.

Proverbs 3:33

By wisdom a house is built,
    and through understanding it is established;
through knowledge its rooms are filled
    with rare and beautiful treasures.

Proverbs 24:3–4

God's Words of Life on
FAMILY

If a widow has children or grandchildren, these should learn first of all to put their religion into practice by caring for their own family and so repaying their parents and grandparents, for this is pleasing to God.... If anyone does not provide for his relatives, and especially for his immediate family, he has denied the faith and is worse than an unbeliever.

1 Timothy 5:4, 8

The house of the righteous stands firm.

Proverbs 12:7

A wife of noble character who can find?
    She is worth far more than rubies.
Her husband has full confidence in her
    and lacks nothing of value....
Her children arise and call her blessed;
    her husband also, and he praises her.

Proverbs 31:10-11, 28

God's Words of Life on
FAMILY

Train a child in the way he should go,
and when he is old he will not turn from it.

Proverbs 22:6

Discipline your son, and he will give you peace;
he will bring delight to your soul.

Proverbs 29:17

The father of a righteous man has great joy;
he who has a wise son delights in him.
May your father and mother be glad;
may she who gave you birth rejoice!

Proverbs 23:24–25

*I have no greater joy than to hear that my children are
walking in the truth.*

3 John 4

The tent of the upright will flourish.

Proverbs 14:11

*Believe in the Lord Jesus, and you will be saved—you
and your household.*

Acts 16:31

Devotional Thought on
FAMILY

If everything else is right but things are in turmoil at home, life becomes very difficult.

That's why so many athletes that we think should be happy because they are so successful in their sport are really quite miserable.

One great athlete who did not succumb to that problem was Anthony Munoz, the former Cincinnati Bengals player who is in the Pro Football Hall of Fame. Munoz was like the man described in Psalm 128. He feared the Lord and put his family at the top of his priority list. The family table at the Munoz home was centered on godly living. As a result, the family had God's blessing.

This is how Munoz made it work: "[My wife and I] really try to make number one in our lives [the fact] that regardless of how many pro bowls you play in, the family and what you did there is what people are going to know you by."

We work hard at jobs, school, and even hobbies. But unless we put in the needed work at home, we may end up finding that when we come home at night, it's all for naught.

Far more important than any success we might have outside the home is the kind of success described in Psalm 128.

That's what makes coming home worth looking forward to.

God's Words of Life on

FOUNDATION

This is what the Sovereign LORD says:
"See, I lay a stone in Zion,
    a tested stone,
a precious cornerstone for a sure foundation;
    the one who trusts will never be dismayed."

Isaiah 28:16

You are no longer foreigners and aliens, but fellow citizens with God's people and members of God's household, built on the foundation of the apostles and prophets, with Christ Jesus himself as the chief cornerstone. In him the whole building is joined together and rises to become a holy temple in the Lord. And in him you too are being built together to become a dwelling in which God lives by his Spirit.

Ephesians 2:19–22

From Judah will come the cornerstone.

Zechariah 10:4

FOUNDATION

If any man builds on this foundation using gold, silver, costly stones, wood, hay or straw, his work will be shown for what it is, because the Day will bring it to light. It will be revealed with fire, and the fire will test the quality of each man's work. If what he has built survives, he will receive his reward.

1 Corinthians 3:12–14

The LORD is my rock, my fortress and my deliverer.
Psalm 18:2

The LORD is exalted, for he dwells on high;
he will fill Zion with justice and righteousness.
He will be the sure foundation for your times,
a rich store of salvation and wisdom and knowledge;
the fear of the LORD is the key to this treasure.
Isaiah 33:5–6

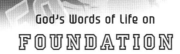

God's Words of Life on

FOUNDATION

As you come to Jesus, the living Stone—rejected by men but chosen by God and precious to him—you also, like living stones, are being built into a spiritual house to be a holy priesthood, offering spiritual sacrifices acceptable to God through Jesus Christ.... Now to you who believe, this stone is precious.

1 Peter 2:4–5, 7

Jesus said, "I will show you what he is like who comes to me and hears my words and puts them into practice. He is like a man building a house, who dug down deep and laid the foundation on rock. When a flood came, the torrent struck that house but could not shake it, because it was well built. But the one who hears my words and does not put them into practice is like a man who built a house on the ground without a foundation. The moment the torrent struck that house, it collapsed and its destruction was complete."

Luke 6:47–49

Who is God besides the LORD?
    And who is the Rock except our God?

Psalm 18:31

God's solid foundation stands firm, sealed with this inscription: "The Lord knows those who are his."

2 Timothy 2:19

Devotional Thought on
FOUNDATION

In baseball, it's pitching. In football, it's a strong defense and a reliable offense. I'm talking about the foundation of success in sports.

Every team that has ever been successful knew what was required in order to achieve success, and the team started building those components.

Always keep in mind that it is possible to build the wrong kind of base. Sometimes baseball teams think they can win on pure power alone, so the management assembles a bunch of sluggers and run scorers—only to find out in the playoffs, or sooner, that their pitching wasn't good enough. They built on the wrong base.

People, like sports teams, do that too. They can build their lives on the wrong foundation—or on no foundation at all. Then, when trouble hits, their lives crumble around them. What they thought was a strong foundation—money, relationships, religion, good deeds, community service, altruism (all good things, by the way)—did not hold them up when things got critical.

In life there can be only one true foundation: Jesus. First Corinthians 3:11 says, "For no one can lay any foundation other than the one already laid, which is Jesus Christ."

Even Christians can be fooled by good things—thinking those things will give them security. But someday that building material will be tested and found inferior.

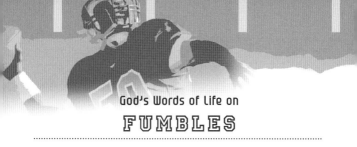

God's Words of Life on

FUMBLES

If someone is caught in a sin, you who are spiritual should restore him gently. But watch yourself, or you also may be tempted. Carry each other's burdens, and in this way you will fulfill the law of Christ.

Galatians 6:1–2

Though I have fallen, I will rise.
Though I sit in darkness,
    the LORD will be my light.
Because I have sinned against him,
    I will bear the LORD's wrath,
until he pleads my case
    and establishes my right.
He will bring me out into the light;
    I will see his righteousness.

Micah 7:8–9

Have mercy on me, O God,
    according to your unfailing love;
according to your great compassion
    blot out my transgressions.
Wash away all my iniquity
    and cleanse me from my sin.

Psalm 51:1–2

FUMBLES

....

Jesus said, "It is not the healthy who need a doctor, but the sick. I have not come to call the righteous, but sinners to repentance."

Luke 5:31–32

Create in me a pure heart, O God,
    and renew a steadfast spirit within me.
Do not cast me from your presence
    or take your Holy Spirit from me.
Restore to me the joy of your salvation
    and grant me a willing spirit, to sustain me.

Psalm 51:10–12

The LORD is compassionate and gracious,
    slow to anger, abounding in love.
He will not always accuse,
    nor will he harbor his anger forever;
he does not treat us as our sins deserve
    or repay us according to our iniquities.
For as high as the heavens are above the earth,
    so great is his love for those who fear him;
as far as the east is from the west,
    so far has he removed our transgressions from us.

Psalm 103:8–12

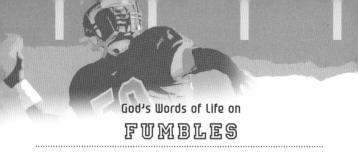

God's Words of Life on

FUMBLES

"Come now, let us reason together,"
    says the LORD.
"Though your sins are like scarlet,
    they shall be as white as snow;
though they are red as crimson,
    they shall be like wool."

Isaiah 1:18

Your righteousness reaches to the skies, O God,
    you who have done great things.
    Who, O God, is like you?
Though you have made me see troubles, many
        and bitter,
    you will restore my life again;
from the depths of the earth
    you will again bring me up.
You will increase my honor
    and comfort me once again.

Psalm 71:19–21

*The God of all grace, who called you to his eternal glory
in Christ, after you have suffered a little while, will himself restore you and make you strong, firm and steadfast.*

1 Peter 5:10

God's Words of Life on
FUMBLES

In my distress I called to the LORD,
and he answered me.
From the depths of the grave I called for help,
and you listened to my cry....
To the roots of the mountains I sank down;
the earth beneath barred me in forever.
But you brought my life up from the pit,
O LORD my God.

Jonah 2:2, 6

This is what the high and lofty One says—
he who lives forever, whose name is holy:
"I live in a high and holy place,
but also with him who is contrite and lowly in spirit,
to revive the spirit of the lowly
and to revive the heart of the contrite."

Isaiah 57:15

You disciplined me like an unruly calf,
and I have been disciplined.
Restore me, and I will return,
because you are the LORD my God.

Jeremiah 31:18

God's Words of Life on

FUMBLES

If we confess our sins, God is faithful and just and will forgive us our sins and purify us from all unrighteousness.

1 John 1:9

Did they stumble so as to fall beyond recovery? Not at all!

Romans 11:11

"If my people, who are called by my name, will humble themselves and pray and seek my face and turn from their wicked ways, then will I hear from heaven and will forgive their sin and will heal their land," declares the LORD.

2 Chronicles 7:14

O LORD, have mercy on me;
   heal me, for I have sinned against you.

Psalm 41:4

If the LORD delights in a man's way,
   he makes his steps firm;
though he stumble, he will not fall,
   for the LORD upholds him with his hand.

Psalm 37:23–24

FUMBLES

....

In the late 1990s, Christians were stunned to find out that a dedicated brother in Christ had stumbled badly on the eve of the biggest sports day of his life. This honored and respected football player made a terrible choice on the night before the Super Bowl, and all Christians felt the reverberations.

One of the teammates of this player was John Burrough, a strong, burly 6'5" 275-pound defensive end. A strong believer in Jesus Christ, Burrough was at first in disbelief concerning his teammate's indiscretion. But he didn't attack his friend for his blunder. Burrough said, "When we found out it was true, every Christian I spoke with immediately prayed for him and his family for a reconciliation of that relationship. He fell flat on his face, but I guarantee he's a better Christian today because of what happened."

When we see a fellow Christian stumble, it's easy to look for opportunities to condemn. Paul, however, suggested that there is a three-part procedure that must be followed—none of which includes criticism.

First, we are to restore that person gently. Restoration is not easy, and it may include confrontation and tears. Second, we need to be careful, lest we stumble on the same problem that tripped up our friend. And third, we need to help our friend carry the burdens of his error.

God's Words of Life on

GLORIFYING GOD

Give thanks to the LORD, call on his name;
    make known among the nations what he has done.
Sing to him, sing praise to him;
    tell of all his wonderful acts.
Glory in his holy name;
    let the hearts of those who seek the LORD rejoice....
Remember the wonders he has done,
    his miracles, and the judgments he pronounced.

1 Chronicles 16:8–10, 12

My mouth will tell of your righteousness,
    of your salvation all day long,
    though I know not its measure.
I will come and proclaim your mighty acts,
      O Sovereign LORD;
    I will proclaim your righteousness, yours alone.
Since my youth, O God, you have taught me,
    and to this day I declare your marvelous deeds.
Even when I am old and gray,
    do not forsake me, O God,
till I declare your power to the next generation,
    your might to all who are to come.

Psalm 71:15–18

Many, O LORD my God,
    are the wonders you have done.
The things you planned for us
    no one can recount to you;
were I to speak and tell of them,
    they would be too many to declare.

Psalm 40:5

GLORIFYING GOD

I will tell of the kindnesses of the LORD,
   the deeds for which he is to be praised,
      according to all the LORD has done for us—
yes, the many good things he has done.

Isaiah 63:7

Be careful, and watch yourselves closely so that you do not forget the things your eyes have seen or let them slip from your heart as long as you live. Teach them to your children and to their children after them.

Deuteronomy 4:9

I will praise you, O LORD, with all my heart;
   I will tell of all your wonders.
I will be glad and rejoice in you;
   I will sing praise to your name, O Most High.

Psalm 9:1–2

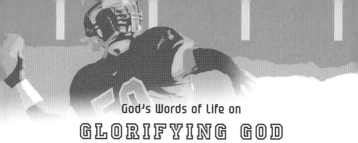

God's Words of Life on

GLORIFYING GOD

Fix these words of mine in your hearts and minds; tie them as symbols on your hands and bind them on your foreheads. Teach them to your children, talking about them when you sit at home and when you walk along the road, when you lie down and when you get up. Write them on the doorframes of your houses and on your gates, so that your days and the days of your children may be many in the land that the LORD swore to give your forefathers, as many as the days that the heavens are above the earth.

Deuteronomy 11:18–21

Great is the LORD and most worthy of praise;
    his greatness no one can fathom.
One generation will commend your works to
      another, O LORD;
    they will tell of your mighty acts.
They will speak of the glorious splendor of your
      majesty,
    and I will meditate on your wonderful works.
They will tell of the power of your awesome works,
    and I will proclaim your great deeds.
They will celebrate your abundant goodness
    and joyfully sing of your righteousness.

Psalm 145:3–7

My tongue will tell of your righteous acts
    all day long, O LORD.

Psalm 71:24

God's Words of Life on
GLORIFYING GOD

Let them give thanks to the LORD for his unfailing love
   and his wonderful deeds for men.
Let them sacrifice thank offerings
   and tell of his works with songs of joy.
Psalm 107:21–22

All you have made will praise you, O LORD;
   your saints will extol you.
They will tell of the glory of your kingdom
   and speak of your might,
so that all men may know of your mighty acts
   and the glorious splendor of your kingdom.
Psalm 145:10–12

Sing praises to the LORD, enthroned in Zion;
   proclaim among the nations what he has done.
Psalm 9:11

I proclaim righteousness in the great assembly;
   I do not seal my lips,
   as you know, O LORD.
I do not hide your righteousness in my heart;
   I speak of your faithfulness and salvation.
I do not conceal your love and your truth
   from the great assembly.
Psalm 40:9–10

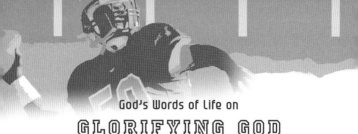

God's Words of Life on
GLORIFYING GOD

Give thanks to the LORD, for he is good;
  his love endures forever.
Who can proclaim the mighty acts of the LORD
  or fully declare his praise?

Psalm 106:1–2

Give thanks to the LORD, call on his name;
  make known among the nations what he has done,
  and proclaim that his name is exalted.
Sing to the LORD, for he has done glorious things;
  let this be known to all the world.

Isaiah 12:4–5

You make me glad by your deeds, O LORD;
  I sing for joy at the works of your hands.
How great are your works, O LORD.

Psalm 92:4–5

Always be prepared to give an answer to everyone who asks you to give the reason for the hope that you have.

1 Peter 3:15

Jesus said, "Whoever acknowledges me before men, the Son of Man will also acknowledge him before the angels of God."

Luke 12:8

Devotional Thought on
GLORIFYING GOD

Thanksgiving and football—it's an American tradition.

On Thanksgiving Day, football is the sport of choice in the United States. Teams such as the Detroit Lions and the Dallas Cowboys traditionally square off against league rivals as the country tunes in.

There's another tradition related to football and TV that is almost as popular as the games themselves: sitting around and talking about the qualities of our favorite teams.

"We've got great linebackers."

"Our quarterback sure knows how to make the big play."

"You can't score off our defense inside the red zone."

When we have a favorite team, we look for good things to brag about.

Imagine what it would be like if we used Thanksgiving Day to do the same thing with God.

"I can't believe how God has seen us through this year!"

"Isn't God's majesty incredible! Just look at the stars on a clear fall night. How can anyone doubt his creative powers?"

"Can you believe he sent Jesus to die for us?"

Let's be honest: We sports fans probably do more bragging about our favorite team and our favorite players than we do about God. Maybe the next time we start talking about sports, we can remember that talking about God and his greatness is a great way to share with others and bring glory to God.

God's Words of Life on

GOD'S CALL

We are God's workmanship, created in Christ Jesus to do good works, which God prepared in advance for us to do.

Ephesians 2:10

Aaron was set apart, he and his descendants forever, to consecrate the most holy things, to offer sacrifices before the Lord, to minister before him and to pronounce blessings in his name forever.

1 Chronicles 23:13

The Lord said to Moses, "I have indeed seen the oppression of my people in Egypt. I have heard their groaning and have come down to set them free. Now come, I will send you back to Egypt."

Acts 7:33–34

The Lord came and stood there, calling as at the other times, "Samuel! Samuel!" Then Samuel said, "Speak, for your servant is listening."

1 Samuel 3:10

God ... has saved us and called us to a holy life—not because of anything we have done but because of his own purpose and grace.

2 Timothy 1:8–9

GOD'S CALL

The word of the LORD came to Jeremiah, saying,
"Before I formed you in the womb I knew you,
before you were born I set you apart."

Jeremiah 1:4–5

The LORD had said to Abram, "Leave your country, your
people and your father's household and go to the land I
will show you."

Genesis 12:1

Jesus went up on a mountainside and called to him
those he wanted, and they came to him. He appointed
twelve—designating them apostles.

Mark 3:13–14

John the Baptist's father Zechariah was filled with the
Holy Spirit and prophesied: ...
"You, my child, will be called a prophet of the
Most High;
for you will go on before the Lord to prepare the
way for him."

Luke 1:67, 76

In a large house there are articles not only of gold and
silver, but also of wood and clay; some are for noble
purposes and some for ignoble. If a man cleanses him-
self from the latter, he will be an instrument for noble
purposes, made holy, useful to the Master and prepared
to do any good work.

2 Timothy 2:20–21

God's Words of Life on
GOD'S CALL

While they were worshiping the Lord and fasting, the Holy Spirit said, "Set apart for me Barnabas and Saul for the work to which I have called them."

Acts 13:2

In Christ we were also chosen, having been predestined according to the plan of him who works out everything in conformity with the purpose of his will, in order that we, who were the first to hope in Christ, might be for the praise of his glory.

Ephesians 1:11

Mordecai told Queen Esther: "Who knows but that you have come to royal position for such a time as this?"

Esther 4:13-14

Therefore, holy brothers, who share in the heavenly calling, fix your thoughts on Jesus, the apostle and high priest whom we confess.

Hebrews 3:1

Then I heard the voice of the Lord saying, "Whom shall I send? And who will go for us?" And I said, "Here am I. Send me!"

Isaiah 6:8

Live a life worthy of the calling you have received.

Ephesians 4:1

Devotional Thought on
GOD'S CALL

Some athletes are set apart for stardom from an early age.

A few years ago, Todd Marinavich burst onto the athletic scene as a quarterback at USC. It was widely known that his father had set him apart to be a quarterback when he was a little boy. His dad trained him in a special way, fed him a special diet (no Big Macs), and instructed him from his youth in the intricacies of being a quarterback.

We who are followers of the truth have been set apart for special work, and we can dedicate ourselves to that task by living as God desires us to live.

In Jeremiah 1:5, we read about the special call God had on Jeremiah's life. Even before Jeremiah was born, God was familiar with Jeremiah and had decided to give him a unique and vital responsibility. Even before Jeremiah's birth, God had designs for him to be a prophet.

In Psalm 139:16, David said that God plans our days before we are even born. Each of us has been especially chosen for a particular work.

It's up to us to follow God's calling and put our hearts and effort behind the work he's called us to do. It's up to us to present ourselves with dedication and sincerity to the one who has designs on our lives.

God's Words of Life on
GOD'S CARE

I lift up my eyes to the hills—
    where does my help come from?
My help comes from the LORD,
    the Maker of heaven and earth.

Psalm 121:1–2

The LORD shielded him and cared for him;
    he guarded him as the apple of his eye,
like an eagle that stirs up its nest
    and hovers over its young,
that spreads its wings to catch them
    and carries them on its pinions.

Deuteronomy 32:10–11

Jesus said, "I am the good shepherd. The good shepherd lays down his life for the sheep. The hired hand is not the shepherd who owns the sheep. So when he sees the wolf coming, he abandons the sheep and runs away. Then the wolf attacks the flock and scatters it. The man runs away because he is a hired hand and cares nothing for the sheep."

John 10:11–13

Hear, O LORD, and answer me,
    for I am poor and needy.
Guard my life, for I am devoted to you.
    You are my God; save your servant
    who trusts in you.

Psalm 86:1–2

God's Words of Life on

GOD'S CARE

....

Fear not, for I have redeemed you;
  I have summoned you by name; you are mine.
When you pass through the waters,
  I will be with you;
and when you pass through the rivers,
  they will not sweep over you.
When you walk through the fire,
  you will not be burned;
  the flames will not set you ablaze,"
    declares the LORD.

Isaiah 43:1–2

No one ever hated his own body, but he feeds and
cares for it, just as Christ does the church—for we are
members of his body.

Ephesians 5:29–30

If you make the Most High your dwelling—
  even the LORD, who is my refuge—
then no harm will befall you,
  no disaster will come near your tent.
For he will command his angels concerning you
  to guard you in all your ways.

Psalm 91:9–11

God's Words of Life on
GOD'S CARE

The LORD watches over you—
  the LORD is your shade at your right hand;
the sun will not harm you by day,
  nor the moon by night.

Psalm 121:5–6

You understand, O LORD;
  remember me and care for me.

Jeremiah 15:15

Abraham took some food and a skin of water and gave them to Hagar. He set them on her shoulders and then sent her off with the boy. She went on her way and wandered in the desert of Beersheba. When the water in the skin was gone, she put the boy under one of the bushes. Then she went off and sat down nearby, about a bowshot away, for she thought, "I cannot watch the boy die." And as she sat there nearby, she began to sob. God heard the boy crying, and the angel of God called to Hagar from heaven and said to her, "What is the matter, Hagar? Do not be afraid; God has heard the boy crying as he lies there. Lift the boy up and take him by the hand, for I will make him into a great nation." Then God opened her eyes and she saw a well of water. So she went and filled the skin with water and gave the boy a drink.

Genesis 21:14–19

God's Words of Life on
GOD'S CARE

The LORD is faithful to all his promises
and loving toward all he has made.
The LORD upholds all those who fall
and lifts up all who are bowed down.
The eyes of all look to you,
and you give them their food at the proper time.
You open your hand
and satisfy the desires of every living thing.
Psalm 145:13–16

Cast all your anxiety on God because he cares for you.
1 Peter 5:7

May the LORD answer you when you are in distress;
may the name of the God of Jacob protect you.
May he send you help from the sanctuary
and grant you support from Zion.
Psalm 20:1–2

*The Lord is near. Do not be anxious about anything, but
in everything, by prayer and petition, with thanksgiving,
present your requests to God. And the peace of God,
which transcends all understanding, will guard your
hearts and your minds in Christ Jesus.*

Philippians 4:5–7

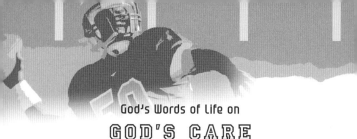

God's Words of Life on

GOD'S CARE

The LORD is good,
    a refuge in times of trouble.
He cares for those who trust in him.

Nahum 1:7

Do not fear, for I am with you;
    do not be dismayed, for I am your God.
I will strengthen you and help you;
    I will uphold you with my righteous right hand.

Isaiah 41:10

Cast your cares on the LORD
    and he will sustain you;
    he will never let the righteous fall.

Psalm 55:22

I will instruct you and teach you in the way you
        should go;
    I will counsel you and watch over you....
Many are the woes of the wicked,
    but the LORD's unfailing love
    surrounds the man who trusts in him.

Psalm 32:8, 10

Devotional Thought on
GOD'S CARE

One thing I don't enjoy when the football season rolls around is the interest everyone has in trying to predict the scores of the weekend's games.

There was no football in Philippi, but there was some predicting going on when Paul and Silas were there. It seems that there was a servant girl who was possessed by a spirit that gave her the ability to tell fortunes. This ability brought in a good income for the girl's owners.

But when Paul saw what was happening, he was deeply disturbed by this clearly demonic activity. So, he cast the demon out of the girl, and suddenly she could no more predict the future than I can tell you who will win the next Super Bowl. Not surprisingly, those who depended on her income were not happy with this new development, and soon Paul and Silas were attacked, beaten, and thrown into jail.

That's when a miraculous thing occurred. Paul and Silas, their backs bleeding and their hearts beating with the tension of the moment, started a mini-revival. They knew the future—they knew that God would always be in control—so they began singing.

Like Paul and Silas, we can predict the future with certainty in this regard: We know that God will always be in control and that he will always take care of us.

God's Words of Life on
GOD'S CONTROL OF THE ACTION

The LORD reigns, let the earth be glad;
let the distant shores rejoice.

Psalm 97:1

"As the rain and the snow
come down from heaven,
and do not return to it
without watering the earth
and making it bud and flourish...
so is my word that goes out from my mouth:
It will not return to me empty,
but will accomplish what I desire
and achieve the purpose for which I sent it,"
declares the LORD.

Isaiah 55:10–11

God does as he pleases
with the powers of heaven
and the peoples of the earth.
No one can hold back his hand
or say to him: "What have you done?"

Daniel 4:35

God's Words of Life on
GOD'S CONTROL OF THE ACTION

O LORD, God of our fathers, are you not the God who is in heaven? You rule over all the kingdoms of the nations. Power and might are in your hand, and no one can withstand you.

2 Chronicles 20:6

The LORD reigns, he is robed in majesty;
    the LORD is robed in majesty
    and is armed with strength.
The world is firmly established;
    it cannot be moved.
Your throne was established long ago;
    you are from all eternity.

Psalm 93:1–2

How great are God's signs,
    how mighty his wonders!
His kingdom is an eternal kingdom;
    his dominion endures from generation to generation.
Daniel 4:3

You are the God who performs miracles;
    you display your power among the peoples.
Psalm 77:14

God's Words of Life on
GOD'S CONTROL OF THE ACTION

God is the King of all the earth;
   sing to him a psalm of praise.
God reigns over the nations;
   God is seated on his holy throne.

Psalm 47:7–8

He is the living God
   and he endures forever;
his kingdom will not be destroyed,
   his dominion will never end.
He rescues and he saves;
   he performs signs and wonders
   in the heavens and on the earth.

Daniel 6:26–27

I know, O LORD, that a man's life is not his own;
   it is not for man to direct his steps.

Jeremiah 10:23

All the days ordained for me
   were written in your book, O LORD,
   before one of them came to be.

Psalm 139:16

Devotional Thought on
GOD'S CONTROL OF THE ACTION

Gill Byrd, former NFL star with the San Diego Chargers, understands uncertainty.

"God is in control of my life," Byrd told *Sports Spectrum* radio in 1993 when he was about to undergo knee surgery that could end his career.

"I'm excited [by] what God is going to do in my life. I'm not at all happy about getting my knee blown out and going through surgery and the pain, but I am excited knowing that he's brought me to this point. I know he doesn't close one door and not open up another."

In fact, God did close the door on Gill Byrd's career with that knee injury. Yet Byrd showed that although his knee was damaged, his heart was strong. He continued to trust God, and he continued to stay close to the sport he loved. He proved that God was still using him when, in 2000, he led Kabeer Gbaja-Biamila of the Green Bay Packers to faith in Jesus Christ.

How do we continue to thrive when we face inner problems like a bad knee or outside forces such as the terrorist threats that became a familiar part of life in the latter half of 2001?

The key is not to lose heart but to focus our eyes above those difficulties and onto Jesus, who is our strength, hope, and help.

God's Words of Life on
GOD'S GAME PLAN

God made known to us the mystery of his will according to his good pleasure, which he purposed in Christ, to be put into effect when the times will have reached their fulfillment—to bring all things in heaven and on earth together under one head, even Christ.

Ephesians 1:9–10

To us a child is born,
    to us a son is given,
    and the government will be on his shoulders.
And he will be called
    Wonderful Counselor, Mighty God,
    Everlasting Father, Prince of Peace.
Of the increase of his government and peace
    there will be no end.
He will reign on David's throne
    and over his kingdom,
establishing and upholding it
    with justice and righteousness
    from that time on and forever.
The zeal of the LORD Almighty
    will accomplish this.

Isaiah 9:6–7

GOD'S GAME PLAN

The plans of the LORD stand firm forever,
  the purposes of his heart through all generations.
Psalm 33:11

Jesus said, "Do not think that I have come to abolish the Law or the Prophets; I have not come to abolish them but to fulfill them. I tell you the truth, until heaven and earth disappear, not the smallest letter, not the least stroke of a pen, will by any means disappear from the Law until everything is accomplished."
Matthew 5:17–18

Do not conform any longer to the pattern of this world, but be transformed by the renewing of your mind. Then you will be able to test and approve what God's will is— his good, pleasing and perfect will.
Romans 12:2

We have not stopped praying for you and asking God to fill you with the knowledge of his will through all spiritual wisdom and understanding. And we pray this in order that you may live a life worthy of the Lord and may please him in every way: bearing fruit in every good work, growing in the knowledge of God, being strengthened with all power according to his glorious might so that you may have great endurance and patience, and joyfully giving thanks to the Father, who has qualified you to share in the inheritance of the saints in the kingdom of light.
Colossians 1:9–12

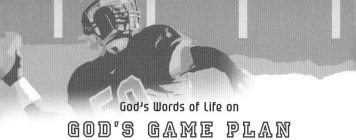

God's Words of Life on
GOD'S GAME PLAN

May the God of peace, who through the blood of the eternal covenant brought back from the dead our Lord Jesus, that great Shepherd of the sheep, equip you with everything good for doing his will, and may he work in us what is pleasing to him, through Jesus Christ, to whom be glory for ever and ever. Amen.

Hebrews 13:20–21

Now listen, you who say, "Today or tomorrow we will go to this or that city, spend a year there, carry on business and make money." Why, you do not even know what will happen tomorrow. What is your life? You are a mist that appears for a little while and then vanishes. Instead, you ought to say, "If it is the Lord's will, we will live and do this or that."

James 4:13–15

Do not boast about tomorrow,
for you do not know what a day may bring forth.

Proverbs 27:1

May the favor of the Lord our God rest upon us;
establish the work of our hands for us—
yes, establish the work of our hands.

Psalm 90:17

Devotional Thought on

GOD'S GAME PLAN

The National Football League and Major League Baseball carefully and logically carved out their schedules for the 2001 football and baseball seasons. Everyone knew on any given day who would be playing where. Reservations were made, tickets were sold, all was in place for each game. Even the play-offs were set—all the way through to the Super Bowl and the World Series.

But then the events of September 11 broke across the 2001 landscape. Along with its horror and its unspeakable tragedies came the little changes in life that accompany such far-reaching events. No longer did those football and baseball schedules make sense. No longer was January 27 Super Bowl Sunday. No longer would the World Series end in October.

Tomorrow is a mystery, the ending of which we do not know. As we face tomorrow, James tells us we first must recognize the will of God in the day's proceedings (James 4:13–17). We can face tomorrow, knowing that it is a gift from God, and we must spend it in a way that pleases him.

We've seen how current events can change everyone's schedules—how we really do not know what tomorrow will bring. That would be a scary thought if we did not live with the recognition that God's will must and shall be accomplished tomorrow.

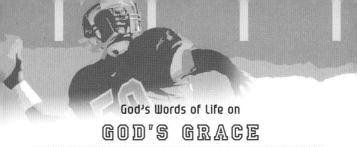

God's Words of Life on
GOD'S GRACE

From the fullness of God's grace we have all received one blessing after another.

John 1:16

Now a righteousness from God, apart from law, has been made known, to which the Law and the Prophets testify. This righteousness from God comes through faith in Jesus Christ to all who believe. There is no difference, for all have sinned and fall short of the glory of God, and are justified freely by his grace through the redemption that came by Christ Jesus.

Romans 3:21–24

Since we have been justified through faith, we have peace with God through our Lord Jesus Christ, through whom we have gained access by faith into this grace in which we now stand.

Romans 5:1–2

Where sin increased, grace increased all the more, so that, just as sin reigned in death, so also grace might reign through righteousness to bring eternal life through Jesus Christ our Lord.

Romans 5:20–21

You know the grace of our Lord Jesus Christ, that though he was rich, yet for your sakes he became poor, so that you through his poverty might become rich.

2 Corinthians 8:9

God's Words of Life on
GOD'S GRACE

....

In Christ we have redemption through his blood, the forgiveness of sins, in accordance with the riches of God's grace that he lavished on us with all wisdom and understanding.

Ephesians 1:7–8

Because of his great love for us, God, who is rich in mercy, made us alive with Christ even when we were dead in transgressions—it is by grace you have been saved. And God raised us up with Christ and seated us with him in the heavenly realms in Christ Jesus, in order that in the coming ages he might show the incomparable riches of his grace, expressed in his kindness to us in Christ Jesus. For it is by grace you have been saved, through faith—and this not from yourselves, it is the gift of God.

Ephesians 2:4–8

We always thank God, the Father of our Lord Jesus Christ, when we pray for you, because we have heard of your faith in Christ Jesus and of the love you have for all the saints—the faith and love that spring from the hope that is stored up for you in heaven and that you have already heard about in the word of truth, the gospel that has come to you. All over the world this gospel is bearing fruit and growing, just as it has been doing among you since the day you heard it and understood God's grace in all its truth.

Colossians 1:3–6

God's Words of Life on

GOD'S GRACE

The grace of God that brings salvation has appeared to all men.

Titus 2:11

When the kindness and love of God our Savior appeared, he saved us, not because of righteous things we had done, but because of his mercy. He saved us through the washing of rebirth and renewal by the Holy Spirit, whom he poured out on us generously through Jesus Christ our Savior, so that, having been justified by his grace, we might become heirs having the hope of eternal life.

Titus 3:4–7

Grace, mercy and peace from God the Father and from Jesus Christ, the Father's Son, will be with us in truth and love.

2 John 1:3

Let us then approach the throne of grace with confidence, so that we may receive mercy and find grace to help us in our time of need.

Hebrews 4:16

The Word became flesh and made his dwelling among us. We have seen his glory, the glory of the One and Only, who came from the Father, full of grace and truth.

John 1:14

Set your hope fully on the grace to be given you when Jesus Christ is revealed.

1 Peter 1:13

Devotional Thought on
GOD'S GRACE

No matter how many times I read Paul's account of his miraculous conversion, I am struck by the contrast between what he was and what he became.

Paul said, "Even though I was once a blasphemer and a persecutor and a violent man, I was shown mercy" (1 Timothy 1:13). Paul was as nasty as he could be, and the only thing that saved him was God's mercy.

When Joe Ehrmann, a former Baltimore Colt, was playing football in the NFL, he had a reputation as a "hardy partyer." Clearly, his interests were solely those that involved finding the next drink and seeking the next thrill.

But then God's mercy captivated his heart. He trusted Jesus as Savior. He became a pastor in Baltimore, and he started an organization that helped get kids off the street and into the family of God.

Football player Irving Fryar went from a man who attacked his wife with a knife to a minister of the gospel.

Is there someone you know who struggles with sin and appears to be headed away from God at the speed of light? That life can be turned around through God's mercy. Perhaps if you were to tell that person about athletes who have escaped sure doom through trusting Jesus, he or she could experience the "grace of our Lord" (1 Timothy 1:14).

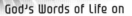

God's Words of Life on

GOD'S PROTECTION

The eyes of the LORD are on those who fear him,
   on those whose hope is in his unfailing love.
Psalm 33:18

Let all who take refuge in you be glad, O LORD;
   let them ever sing for joy.
Spread your protection over them,
   that those who love your name may rejoice in you.
Psalm 5:11

O LORD, you will keep us safe.
Psalm 12:7

Guard my life and rescue me, O LORD;
   let me not be put to shame,
   for I take refuge in you.
May integrity and uprightness protect me,
   because my hope is in you.
Psalm 25:20–21

Do not withhold your mercy from me, O LORD;
   may your love and your truth always protect me.
Psalm 40:11

God's Words of Life on
GOD'S PROTECTION

As for God, his way is perfect;
   the word of the LORD is flawless.
He is a shield
   for all who take refuge in him.

2 Samuel 22:31

In God I trust; I will not be afraid.
   What can man do to me?

Psalm 56:11

Blessed is he who has regard for the weak;
   the LORD delivers him in times of trouble.
The LORD will protect him and preserve his life;
   he will bless him in the land.

Psalm 41:1–2

"Because he loves me," says the LORD, "I will rescue him;
   I will protect him, for he acknowledges my name.
He will call upon me, and I will answer him;
   I will be with him in trouble,
   I will deliver him and honor him.
With long life will I satisfy him
   and show him my salvation."

Psalm 91:14–16

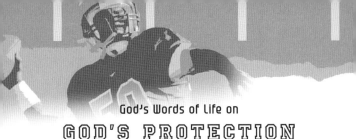

God's Words of Life on
GOD'S PROTECTION

The LORD is my rock, my fortress and my deliverer;
   my God is my rock, in whom I take refuge,
   my shield and the horn of my salvation.
He is my stronghold, my refuge and my savior.

2 Samuel 22:2–3

The LORD will keep you from all harm—
   he will watch over your life;
the LORD will watch over your coming and going
   both now and forevermore.

Psalm 121:7–8

There is no one like the God of Jeshurun,
   who rides on the heavens to help you
   and on the clouds in his majesty.
The eternal God is your refuge,
   and underneath are the everlasting arms.

Deuteronomy 33:26–27

*Jesus prayed for his disciples: "Holy Father, protect
them by the power of your name—the name you gave
me—so that they may be one as we are one. While I
was with them, I protected them and kept them safe by
that name you gave me.... My prayer is not that you
take them out of the world but that you protect them
from the evil one."*

John 17:11–12, 15

GOD'S PROTECTION

Taste and see that the LORD is good;
blessed is the man who takes refuge in him.

Psalm 34:8

The LORD is gracious and righteous;
our God is full of compassion.
The LORD protects the simplehearted;
when I was in great need, he saved me.

Psalm 116:5–6

Keep me safe, O God,
for in you I take refuge.

Psalm 16:1

God will not let your foot slip—
he who watches over you will not slumber;
indeed, he who watches over Israel
will neither slumber nor sleep.

Psalm 121:3–4

*May you be richly rewarded by the LORD, the God of
Israel, under whose wings you have come to take refuge.*

Ruth 2:12

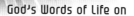

God's Words of Life on

GOD'S PROTECTION

The LORD is my light and my salvation—
  whom shall I fear?
The LORD is the stronghold of my life—
  of whom shall I be afraid?

Psalm 27:1

O LORD, you have been a refuge for the poor,
  a refuge for the needy in his distress,
a shelter from the storm
  and a shade from the heat.

Isaiah 25:4

The salvation of the righteous comes from the LORD;
  he is their stronghold in time of trouble.

Psalm 37:39

He who fears the LORD has a secure fortress,
  and for his children it will be a refuge.

Proverbs 14:26

*Jesus said, "My sheep listen to my voice; I know them,
and they follow me. I give them eternal life, and they
shall never perish; no one can snatch them out of my
hand. My Father, who has given them to me, is greater
than all; no one can snatch them out of my Father's
hand. I and the Father are one."*

John 10:27–30

Devotional Thought on
GOD'S PROTECTION

Imagine the horror Jeremiah must have faced as he watched the Babylonians bear down on his beloved country. He knew they had burned the royal palace and torn down the walls of Jerusalem. As they advanced toward him, Jeremiah must have felt the hot breath of Babylonian danger, wondering what would happen to him.

But when the Babylonians reached Jeremiah, he was as safe as a quarterback at practice. It was like he had the quarterback's red shirt on because he remained unharmed. Just like a quarterback is off-limits to the defensive linemen during practice, Jeremiah was off-limits to the attacking Babylonians.

Why did Jeremiah get the quarterback-in-practice treatment? For one simple reason: He trusted God.

While all around him the people of Judah thumbed their noses at God's guidelines for living, Jeremiah stood strong in obedience. And for that God protected him.

Now, we can't make the assumption from this episode that if we obey God and always strive to please him, God will keep the advancing defenders from throwing us for a loss. But we do know that, ultimately, those of us who have put our faith and trust in Christ face no foe that can rip us out of God's hands.

God has promised us constant companionship and eternal protection. And that's even better than being protected from the marauding Babylonian hordes.

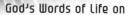

God's Words of Life on
GOOD JUDGMENT

Preserve sound judgment and discernment,
   do not let them out of your sight;
they will be life for you,
   an ornament to grace your neck.
Then you will go on your way in safety,
   and your foot will not stumble;
when you lie down, you will not be afraid;
   when you lie down, your sleep will be sweet.

Proverbs 3:21–24

Wisdom is supreme; therefore get wisdom.
   Though it cost all you have, get understanding.
Esteem her, and she will exalt you;
   embrace her, and she will honor you.
She will set a garland of grace on your head
   and present you with a crown of splendor.

Proverbs 4:7–9

My son, pay attention to my wisdom,
   listen well to my words of insight,
that you may maintain discretion
   and your lips may preserve knowledge.

Proverbs 5:1–2

God's Words of Life on
GOOD JUDGMENT

Wisdom reposes in the heart of the discerning.
Proverbs 14:33

My son, keep my words
    and store up my commands within you.
Keep my commands and you will live;
    guard my teachings as the apple of your eye.
Bind them on your fingers;
    write them on the tablet of your heart.
Say to wisdom, "You are my sister,"
    and call understanding your kinsman.
Proverbs 7:1–4

A man is praised according to his wisdom.
Proverbs 12:8

Knowledge comes easily to the discerning.
Proverbs 14:6

The wisdom of the prudent is to give thought to their ways.
Proverbs 14:8

God's Words of Life on

GOOD JUDGMENT

Do good to your servant
  according to your word, O LORD.
Teach me knowledge and good judgment,
  for I believe in your commands.

Psalm 119:65–66

A man of understanding keeps a straight course.

Proverbs 15:21

How much better to get wisdom than gold,
  to choose understanding rather than silver!

Proverbs 16:16

The fountain of wisdom is a bubbling brook.

Proverbs 18:4

Buy the truth and do not sell it;
  get wisdom, discipline and understanding.

Proverbs 23:23

Wisdom is sweet to your soul;
  if you find it, there is a future hope for you,
  and your hope will not be cut off.

Proverbs 24:14

God's Words of Life on
GOOD JUDGMENT

Blessed is the man who finds wisdom,
   the man who gains understanding,
for she is more profitable than silver
   and yields better returns than gold.
She is more precious than rubies;
   nothing you desire can compare with her.
Long life is in her right hand;
   in her left hand are riches and honor.
Her ways are pleasant ways,
   and all her paths are peace.
She is a tree of life to those who embrace her;
   those who lay hold of her will be blessed.

Proverbs 3:13–18

He who walks in wisdom is kept safe.

Proverbs 28:26

Wisdom is better than folly,
   just as light is better than darkness.

Ecclesiastes 2:13

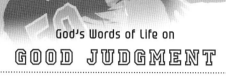

God's Words of Life on
GOOD JUDGMENT

To the man who pleases him, God gives wisdom, knowledge and happiness.

Ecclesiastes 2:26

Wisdom, like an inheritance, is a good thing
 and benefits those who see the sun.

Ecclesiastes 7:11

Jesus said, "Be as shrewd as snakes and as innocent as doves."

Matthew 10:16

The man without the Spirit does not accept the things that come from the Spirit of God, for they are foolishness to him, and he cannot understand them, because they are spiritually discerned. The spiritual man makes judgments about all things.

1 Corinthians 2:14–15

We have conducted ourselves in the world, and especially in our relations with you, in the holiness and sincerity that are from God. We have done so not according to worldly wisdom but according to God's grace.

2 Corinthians 1:12

The fear of the Lord—that is wisdom,
 and to shun evil is understanding.

Job 28:28

Devotional Thought on
GOOD JUDGMENT

Remember this old saying you might have heard your parents repeat: "Nothing good ever happens after midnight"? That should be put on a plaque and hung on the wall of every locker room in the country.

Far too often, we hear of athletes who are in the wrong place at the wrong time—putting their careers in jeopardy because of it.

The book of Proverbs speaks of the kinds of poor decisions these really good athletes make. It suggests that a person who lives by wisdom's guidance will be saved from the "ways of wicked men" (Proverbs 2:12).

Funny thing is, it's not hard to discern who "wicked men" are. In fact, some leagues have special seminars for rookies to help them learn what types of people and situations to avoid.

If the new players need some help, we can suggest Proverbs 2:12–14 to them. Here are the kinds of people one should avoid:

Those "whose words are perverse."

Those who "leave the straight paths to walk in dark ways."

Those who "delight in doing wrong."

The next time you read about an athlete who stumbled into trouble, remind yourself of these verses. It is vital that you steer clear of those who might lead you in a direction that neither you nor God wants you to take.

God's Words of Life on
HARD HITS

Who shall separate us from the love of Christ? Shall trouble or hardship or persecution or famine or nakedness or danger or sword? ...No, in all these things we are more than conquerors through him who loved us. For I am convinced that neither death nor life, neither angels nor demons, neither the present nor the future, nor any powers, neither height nor depth, nor anything else in all creation, will be able to separate us from the love of God that is in Christ Jesus our Lord.

Romans 8:35, 37–39

Blessed is the man who perseveres under trial, because when he has stood the test, he will receive the crown of life that God has promised to those who love him.

James 1:12

Help us, O LORD our God, for we rely on you.

2 Chronicles 14:11

Give ear to my words, O LORD,
    consider my sighing.
Listen to my cry for help,
    my King and my God,
    for to you I pray.

Psalm 5:1–2

God's Words of Life on
HARD HITS

The LORD gives strength to the weary,
and increases the power of the weak.
Even youths grow tired and weary,
and young men stumble and fall;
but those who hope in the LORD
will renew their strength.
They will soar on wings like eagles;
they will run and not grow weary,
they will walk and not be faint.

Isaiah 40:29–31

Turn, O LORD, and deliver me;
save me because of your unfailing love.

Psalm 6:4

The cords of death entangled me;
the torrents of destruction overwhelmed me.
The cords of the grave coiled around me;
the snares of death confronted me.
In my distress I called to the LORD;
I cried to my God for help.
From his temple he heard my voice;
my cry came before him, into his ears.

Psalm 18:4–6

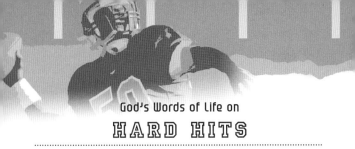

God's Words of Life on
HARD HITS

We wait in hope for the LORD;
he is our help and our shield.
In him our hearts rejoice,
for we trust in his holy name.
May your unfailing love rest upon us, O LORD,
even as we put our hope in you.

Psalm 33:20–22

Hear my cry for mercy
as I call to you for help,
as I lift up my hands
toward your Most Holy Place.

Psalm 28:2

O LORD my God, I called to you for help
and you healed me.
O LORD, you brought me up from the grave;
you spared me from going down into the pit.

Psalm 30:2–3

The LORD reached down from on high and took hold
of me;
he drew me out of deep waters....
He brought me out into a spacious place;
he rescued me because he delighted in me.

Psalm 18:16, 19

Devotional Thought on
HARD HITS

Roger Staubach, who quarterbacked the Dallas Cowboys during the late 1970s and early 1980s, led the 'Boys to the Super Bowl in 1972 and 1978. On his way to a Hall of Fame career, Staubach didn't always have an easy road of it. He had his share of concussions and other injuries. He had to learn to get back up after being knocked down.

A dedicated Christian, Staubach knows that we all face in real life what he faced on the field: oppositions and setbacks. "[Second Corinthians 4:8–9] says we are oppressed on every side by troubles, but not crushed and broken. We are perplexed because we don't know why things happen as they do. But we don't give up and quit. We are hunted down; God never abandons us. We get knocked down, but we get up again. And we keep on going. Perseverance is essential, I think, to deal with life."

Is it ever!

Life often seems like it is blitzing us from all sides. But we cannot be crushed or broken. We have on our side the most powerful entity in the universe—a holy, almighty God. That fact reminds us that nothing can defeat us in the long run. We can persevere because we know the outcome. We may be down, but we are never out of this game.

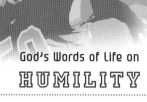

God's Words of Life on
HUMILITY

*Jesus said, "The greatest among you will be your servant.
For whoever exalts himself will be humbled, and whoever humbles himself will be exalted."*

Matthew 23:11–12

Jesus said, "Blessed are the meek,
     for they will inherit the earth."

Matthew 5:5

A man's pride brings him low,
     but a man of lowly spirit gains honor.

Proverbs 29:23

*Think of what you were when you were called. Not
many of you were wise by human standards; not many
were influential; not many were of noble birth. But God
chose the foolish things of the world to shame the wise;
God chose the weak things of the world to shame the
strong. He chose the lowly things of this world and the
despised things—and the things that are not—to nullify
the things that are, so that no one may boast before
him. It is because of him that you are in Christ Jesus,
who has become for us wisdom from God—that is, our
righteousness, holiness and redemption. Therefore, as
it is written: "Let him who boasts boast in the Lord."*

1 Corinthians 1:26–31

God's Words of Life on
HUMILITY

"Let not the wise man boast of his wisdom
   or the strong man boast of his strength
   or the rich man boast of his riches,
but let him who boasts boast about this:
   that he understands and knows me,"
      declares the LORD.

Jeremiah 9:23–24

*"If my people, who are called by my name, will humble
themselves and pray and seek my face and turn from their
wicked ways, then will I hear from heaven and will forgive
their sin and will heal their land," declares the LORD.*

2 Chronicles 7:14

You save the humble, O LORD,
   but bring low those whose eyes are haughty.

Psalm 18:27

Humble yourselves before the Lord, and he will lift you up.

James 4:10

Though the LORD is on high, he looks upon the lowly,
   but the proud he knows from afar.

Psalm 138:6

God's Words of Life on
HUMILITY

Humility comes before honor.

Proverbs 15:33

The LORD guides the humble in what is right
and teaches them his way.

Psalm 25:9

*God has brought down rulers from their thrones
but has lifted up the humble.*

Luke 1:52

*Clothe yourselves with humility toward one another,
because,*

"*God opposes the proud
but gives grace to the humble.*"
*Humble yourselves, therefore, under God's mighty
hand, that he may lift you up in due time.*

1 Peter 5:5–6

The LORD sustains the humble
but casts the wicked to the ground.

Psalm 147:6

Better to be lowly in spirit and among the oppressed
than to share plunder with the proud.

Proverbs 16:19

God's Words of Life on
HUMILITY

The LORD takes delight in his people;
   he crowns the humble with salvation.

Psalm 149:4

*Do not think of yourself more highly than you ought,
but rather think of yourself with sober judgment, in
accordance with the measure of faith God has given you.*

Romans 12:3

Humility and the fear of the LORD
   bring wealth and honor and life.

Proverbs 22:4

When pride comes, then comes disgrace,
   but with humility comes wisdom.

Proverbs 11:2

*Live in harmony with one another; be sympathetic, love
as brothers, be compassionate and humble.*

1 Peter 3:8

The meek will inherit the land
   and enjoy great peace.

Psalm 37:11

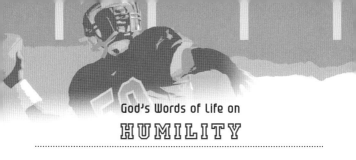

God's Words of Life on

HUMILITY

My heart is not proud, O LORD,
　　my eyes are not haughty;
I do not concern myself with great matters
　　or things too wonderful for me.
But I have stilled and quieted my soul;
　　like a weaned child with its mother,
　　like a weaned child is my soul within me.

Psalm 131:1–2

*Everything God does is right and all his ways are just.
And those who walk in pride he is able to humble.*

Daniel 4:37

*Jesus said, "Come to me, all you who are weary and
burdened, and I will give you rest. Take my yoke upon
you and learn from me, for I am gentle and humble in
heart, and you will find rest for your souls."*

Matthew 11:28–29

Devotional Thought on
𝕳𝕌𝕸𝕀𝕃𝕀𝕋𝕐

There are athletes who attempt to live by Paul's admonition to "do nothing out of selfish ambition or vain conceit, but in humility consider others better than yourselves" (Philippians 2:3).

For instance, longtime NFL kicker Jason Hanson, when asked about money and pro athletes, once told me, "I find that God is teaching us the very same things you learn if you don't have money. Whether you are rich or poor, the same shaping by God takes place. I hope I'm humble."

And Earnest Byner, a former NFL runningback, told me, "The Bible speaks about bragging, and it says let other people talk good about you."

Life is lived better and more effectively if we carry on without bragging, which gets us back to what Paul was talking about. Our efforts to live in humility have this basis: Jesus—the all-time greatest person who ever lived—humbled himself by coming to earth and living among mere humans.

Jesus didn't just make himself human—he made himself less than that. Jesus "made himself nothing" (Philippians 2:7).

So here's the comparison: Jesus, the sinless one, the creator of the universe and the Savior of the world, considers himself nothing. Christians, the sinful ones, the citizens of God's universe and the ones Jesus died for—what should we consider ourselves?

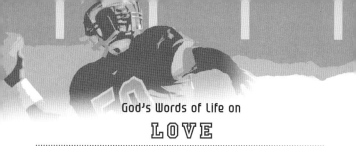

God's Words of Life on

LOVE

Let no debt remain outstanding, except the continuing debt to love one another, for he who loves his fellowman has fulfilled the law. The commandments, "Do not commit adultery," "Do not murder," "Do not steal," "Do not covet," and whatever other commandment there may be, are summed up in this one rule: "Love your neighbor as yourself." Love does no harm to its neighbor. Therefore love is the fulfillment of the law.

Romans 13:8–10

What a man desires is unfailing love.

Proverbs 19:22

No one has ever seen God; but if we love one another, God lives in us and his love is made complete in us.

1 John 4:12

Many waters cannot quench love;
    rivers cannot wash it away.
If one were to give
    all the wealth of his house for love,
    it would be utterly scorned.

Song of Songs 8:7

He who pursues righteousness and love
    finds life, prosperity and honor.

Proverbs 21:21

God's Words of Life on
LOVE

Love builds up.

1 Corinthians 8:1

To love God with all your heart, with all your under-standing and with all your strength, and to love your neighbor as yourself is more important than all burnt offerings and sacrifices.

Mark 12:33

Love must be sincere.

Romans 12:9

If I speak in the tongues of men and of angels, but have not love, I am only a resounding gong or a clanging cymbal. If I have the gift of prophecy and can fathom all mysteries and all knowledge, and if I have a faith that can move mountains, but have not love, I am nothing. If I give all I possess to the poor and surrender my body to the flames, but have not love, I gain nothing.

1 Corinthians 13:1–3

God is love. Whoever lives in love lives in God, and God in him. In this way, love is made complete among us so that we will have confidence on the day of judg-ment, because in this world we are like him.

1 John 4:16–17

Love covers over all wrongs.

Proverbs 10:12

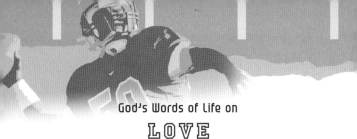

God's Words of Life on
LOVE

The only thing that counts is faith expressing itself through love.

Galatians 5:6

Love is patient, love is kind. It does not envy, it does not boast, it is not proud. It is not rude, it is not self-seeking, it is not easily angered, it keeps no record of wrongs. Love does not delight in evil but rejoices with the truth. It always protects, always trusts, always hopes, always perseveres. Love never fails.

1 Corinthians 13:4–8

May the Lord make your love increase and overflow for each other and for everyone else, just as ours does for you. May he strengthen your hearts so that you will be blameless and holy in the presence of our God and Father when our Lord Jesus comes with all his holy ones.

1 Thessalonians 3:12–13

There is no fear in love. But perfect love drives out fear.

1 John 4:18

Your love has given me great joy and encouragement, because you, brother, have refreshed the hearts of the saints.

Philemon 7

God's Words of Life on
LOVE

These three remain: faith, hope and love. But the greatest of these is love.

1 Corinthians 13:13

Speaking the truth in love, we will in all things grow up into him who is the Head, that is, Christ. From him the whole body, joined and held together by every supporting ligament, grows and builds itself up in love, as each part does its work.

Ephesians 4:15–16

Follow the way of love.

1 Corinthians 14:1

We ought always to thank God for you, brothers, and rightly so, because your faith is growing more and more, and the love every one of you has for each other is increasing.

2 Thessalonians 1:3

Those who plan what is good find love and faithfulness.

Proverbs 14:22

We love because God first loved us.

1 John 4:19

Keep on loving each other as brothers.

Hebrews 13:1

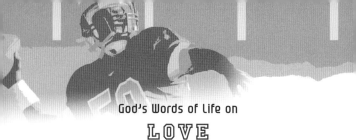

God's Words of Life on
LOVE

Do everything in love.

1 Corinthians 16:14

Greet one another with a kiss of love.

1 Peter 5:14

You yourselves have been taught by God to love each other.

1 Thessalonians 4:9

This is God's command: to believe in the name of his Son, Jesus Christ, and to love one another as he commanded us.

1 John 3:23

Above all, love each other deeply.

1 Peter 4:8

Whoever loves God must also love his brother.

1 John 4:21

God's command is that you walk in love.

2 John 6

Jesus said, "My command is this: Love each other as I have loved you. Greater love has no one than this, that he lay down his life for his friends."

John 15:12–13

Devotional Thought on
LOVE

David Forester had been battling for a long time to become the top kicker on his college football team. Injuries had held him back, but as he entered his senior year at the University of California-Davis, he appeared ready to step into the spotlight.

But then his little brother, Tommy, had a setback in his battle with kidney problems. Tests were done to see who could donate a new kidney.

It was David.

But if he were to give up his kidney so close to the football season, he would never recover in time to compete.

It didn't matter. This was his brother.

David said, "It was never a hard decision to make. The closer you walk with the Lord—and I've been really close to him through this process—the more you see that his plan becomes your plan."

He gave up his kidney—and his final year of football—so his brother could have a new lease on a healthy life.

John told us a long time ago how neat a brother's love can be: "Whoever loves his brother lives in the light, and there is nothing in him to make him stumble" (1 John 2:10).

Our brothers and sisters in Jesus Christ—our adopted siblings through our Father God—need our sacrificial love. And when they get it, we are the true beneficiaries.

God's Words of Life on

MOTIVATION

Let us draw near to God with a sincere heart in full assurance of faith.... Let us hold unswervingly to the hope we profess, for he who promised is faithful. And let us consider how we may spur one another on toward love and good deeds.

Hebrews 10:22–24

Acknowledge the God of your father, and serve him with wholehearted devotion and with a willing mind, for the LORD searches every heart and understands every motive behind the thoughts.

1 Chronicles 28:9

Devote yourself to the public reading of Scripture, to preaching and to teaching.... Be diligent in these matters; give yourself wholly to them, so that everyone may see your progress. Watch your life and doctrine closely. Persevere in them, because if you do, you will save both yourself and your hearers.

1 Timothy 4:13, 15–16

Do not throw away your confidence; it will be richly rewarded. You need to persevere so that when you have done the will of God, you will receive what he has promised.

Hebrews 10:35–36

Be sure to fear the LORD and serve him faithfully with all your heart; consider what great things he has done for you.

1 Samuel 12:24

God's Words of Life on
MOTIVATION

Let us not become weary in doing good, for at the proper time we will reap a harvest if we do not give up.
Galatians 6:9

Devote your heart and soul to seeking the LORD your God.
1 Chronicles 22:19

I press on to take hold of that for which Christ Jesus took hold of me. Brothers, I do not consider myself yet to have taken hold of it. But one thing I do: Forgetting what is behind and straining toward what is ahead, I press on toward the goal to win the prize for which God has called me heavenward in Christ Jesus.
Philippians 3:12–14

We always thank God for all of you, mentioning you in our prayers. We continually remember before our God and Father your work produced by faith, your labor prompted by love, and your endurance inspired by hope in our Lord Jesus Christ.
1 Thessalonians 1:2–3

Your hearts must be fully committed to the LORD our God, to live by his decrees and obey his commands.
1 Kings 8:61

God's Words of Life on

MOTIVATION

Motives are weighed by the LORD.

Proverbs 16:2

You alone, O LORD, know the hearts of all men.

1 Kings 8:39

I know, my God, that you test the heart and are pleased with integrity.

1 Chronicles 29:17

Lord, you know everyone's heart.

Acts 1:24

The Lord will bring to light what is hidden in darkness and will expose the motives of men's hearts. At that time each will receive his praise from God.

1 Corinthians 4:5

The LORD does not look at the things man looks at. Man looks at the outward appearance, but the LORD looks at the heart.

1 Samuel 16:7

God's Words of Life on
MOTIVATION

May the words of my mouth and the meditation of
    my heart
  be pleasing in your sight,
  O Lord, my Rock and my Redeemer.

Psalm 19:14

Test me, O Lord, and try me,
    examine my heart and my mind;
for your love is ever before me,
    and I walk continually in your truth.

Psalm 26:2–3

God knows the secrets of the heart.

Psalm 44:21

Search me, O God, and know my heart;
    test me and know my anxious thoughts.
See if there is any offensive way in me,
    and lead me in the way everlasting.

Psalm 139:23–24

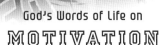

God's Words of Life on

MOTIVATION

The crucible for silver and the furnace for gold,
but the LORD tests the heart.

Proverbs 17:3

As water reflects a face,
so a man's heart reflects the man.

Proverbs 27:19

Jesus said, "Blessed are the pure in heart,
for they will see God."

Matthew 5:8

Jesus said, "God knows your hearts."

Luke 16:15

*Jesus said, "I am he who searches hearts and minds, and
I will repay each of you according to your deeds."*

Revelation 2:23

*Whatever you do, work at it with all your heart, as work-
ing for the Lord, not for men, since you know that you
will receive an inheritance from the Lord as a reward. It
is the Lord Christ you are serving.*

Colossians 3:23–24

Devotional Thought on
MOTIVATION

"Dear Lord, help us win this game."

Bobby Bowden, the legendary coach of the Florida State Seminoles, was always known for his faith in God and his godliness. And Bobby Bowden was noted for being a coach who prayed. But he didn't pray prayers like that one.

"I start each coaching session with Bible reading, devotion, and prayer," said the master coach. "I tell our coaches I want to use it as a time to ask God to give us guidance. I don't believe God's going to make us win. I don't pray for that. But we just ask him to give us wisdom in decisions we have to make. And to show us how to teach our boys to do their best and things like that."

James said, "When you ask, you do not receive, because you ask with wrong motives" (James 4:3). Coach was afraid of doing that, so he confined his prayers to asking for wisdom and for guidance in teaching his charges.

How often do we check our motives before we pray? Do we sometimes pray selfishly, focusing on ourselves rather than on the God of the universe? If so, even if we are not praying for our team to beat the University of Florida, we are praying with motives that God cannot honor.

God's Words of Life on

OBEYING THE COACH

This is love: that we walk in obedience to God's commands.

2 John 6

"You must obey my laws and be careful to follow my decrees. I am the LORD your God. Keep my decrees and laws, for the man who obeys them will live by them. I am the LORD."

Leviticus 18:4–5

The LORD commanded us to obey all these decrees and to fear the LORD our God, so that we might always prosper.... And if we are careful to obey all this law before the LORD our God, as he has commanded us, that will be our righteousness.

Deuteronomy 6:24–25

Jesus said, "Blessed ... are those who hear the word of God and obey it."

Luke 11:28

Jesus said, "If you obey my commands, you will remain in my love, just as I have obeyed my Father's commands and remain in his love."

John 15:10

Although Jesus was a son, he learned obedience from what he suffered and, once made perfect, he became the source of eternal salvation for all who obey him.

Hebrews 5:8–9

God's Words of Life on

OBEYING THE COACH

....

It is not those who hear the law who are righteous in God's sight, but it is those who obey the law who will be declared righteous.

Romans 2:13

Anyone who listens to the word but does not do what it says is like a man who looks at his face in a mirror and, after looking at himself, goes away and immediately forgets what he looks like. But the man who looks intently into the perfect law that gives freedom, and continues to do this, not forgetting what he has heard, but doing it—he will be blessed in what he does.

James 1:23–25

"Follow my decrees and be careful to obey my laws, and you will live safely in the land," declares the LORD.

Leviticus 25:18

Jesus said, "If anyone loves me, he will obey my teaching. My Father will love him, and we will come to him and make our home with him."

John 14:23

"We will do everything the LORD has said; we will obey."

Exodus 24:7

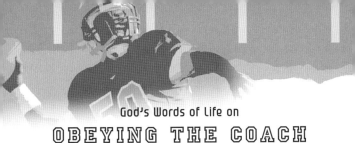

God's Words of Life on

OBEYING THE COACH

It is the LORD your God you must follow, and him you must revere. Keep his commands and obey him; serve him and hold fast to him.

Deuteronomy 13:4

Be very careful to keep the commandment and the law that Moses the servant of the LORD gave you: to love the LORD your God, to walk in all his ways, to obey his commands, to hold fast to him and to serve him with all your heart and all your soul.

Joshua 22:5

To obey is better than sacrifice.

1 Samuel 15:22

Your statutes, O LORD, are my heritage forever;
    they are the joy of my heart.
My heart is set on keeping your decrees
    to the very end.

Psalm 119:111–112

From everlasting to everlasting
    the LORD's love is with those who fear him,
    and his righteousness with their children's children—
with those who keep his covenant
    and remember to obey his precepts.

Psalm 103:17–18

Devotional Thought on

OBEYING THE COACH

Several years ago, Notre Dame University opened its remodeled football stadium on a sunny, warm summer afternoon as the Fighting Irish took on the Georgia Tech Yellow Jackets.

It was a great afternoon except for one thing. There was a water main break somewhere in the stadium, so there was no running water. Well, there was some running water, but it was running in all the wrong places—like all over the floor in the restrooms.

Moses ran up against some water that caused him some big problems too (Numbers 20:1–13). But this wasn't a plumbing problem. It was a heart problem—Moses' heart.

When he and the people arrived at Kadesh, they were thirsty. But Kadesh was dry.

God gave Moses strict instructions about how to fix this water problem. But Moses did what we all do. He decided to try his own method instead of following the designer's directions. Because of his grace, God let the water come to refresh the people, but because of his sense of right and wrong, God punished Moses, whose actions had drawn attention to himself rather than to God. So God told him that he would not see the Promised Land.

There's nothing better for us to do than to obey God's instructions and trust his wisdom. Anything else just brings a flood of trouble.

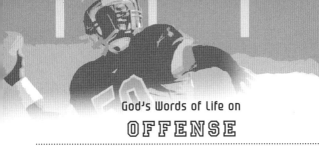

God's Words of Life on
OFFENSE

Jesus said, "Go and make disciples of all nations, baptizing them in the name of the Father and of the Son and of the Holy Spirit, and teaching them to obey everything I have commanded you. And surely I am with you always, to the very end of the age."

Matthew 28:19–20

Jesus commanded us to preach to the people and to testify that he is the one whom God appointed as judge of the living and the dead.

Acts 10:42

Day after day, in the temple courts and from house to house, the apostles never stopped teaching and proclaiming the good news that Jesus is the Christ.

Acts 5:42

It has always been my ambition to preach the gospel where Christ was not known.... As it is written:

"Those who were not told about him will see,
    and those who have not heard will understand."

Romans 15:20–21

With great power the apostles continued to testify to the resurrection of the Lord Jesus, and much grace was upon them all.

Acts 4:33

God's Words of Life on

OFFENSE

Jesus said, "You will receive power when the Holy Spirit comes on you; and you will be my witnesses in Jerusalem, and in all Judea and Samaria, and to the ends of the earth."

Acts 1:8

Though I am free and belong to no man, I make myself a slave to everyone, to win as many as possible. To the Jews I became like a Jew, to win the Jews. To those under the law I became like one under the law (though I myself am not under the law), so as to win those under the law. To those not having the law I became like one not having the law (though I am not free from God's law but am under Christ's law), so as to win those not having the law. To the weak I became weak, to win the weak. I have become all things to all men so that by all possible means I might save some. I do all this for the sake of the gospel, that I may share in its blessings.

1 Corinthians 9:19–23

We have seen and testify that the Father has sent his Son to be the Savior of the world. If anyone acknowledges that Jesus is the Son of God, God lives in him and he in God.

1 John 4:14–15

The message of the cross is foolishness to those who are perishing, but to us who are being saved it is the power of God.

1 Corinthians 1:18

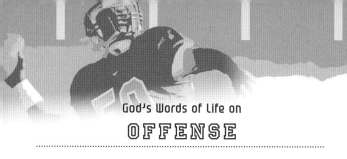

God's Words of Life on
OFFENSE

Jesus said to his disciples, "Go into all the world and preach the good news to all creation. Whoever believes and is baptized will be saved."

Mark 16:15–16

We do not preach ourselves, but Jesus Christ as Lord, and ourselves as your servants for Jesus' sake. For God, who said, "Let light shine out of darkness," made his light shine in our hearts to give us the light of the knowledge of the glory of God in the face of Christ.

2 Corinthians 4:5–6

I became a servant of this gospel by the gift of God's grace given me through the working of his power.

Ephesians 3:7

We speak as men approved by God to be entrusted with the gospel. We are not trying to please men but God, who tests our hearts.

1 Thessalonians 2:4

How, then, can they call on the one they have not believed in? And how can they believe in the one of whom they have not heard? And how can they hear without someone preaching to them? And how can they preach unless they are sent? As it is written, "How beautiful are the feet of those who bring good news!"

Romans 10:14–15

Devotional Thought on
OFFENSE

It seems like an oxymoron, doesn't it? How can feet be beautiful?

Well, we could say that Jason Hanson and Gary Anderson have feet that were beautiful to their teammates, because they were two of the NFL's premier field goal kickers.

Or perhaps we could single out the feet of World Cup and Olympic soccer star Michelle Akers. Maybe Kriss Akabusi of Great Britain has beautiful feet because he's been an Olympic runner. Or maybe Jonathan Edwards, also from Great Britain, has beautiful feet because he broke the world record for the triple jump. Could we say Napoleon Kaufman had beautiful feet during his days of carrying the ball for the Oakland Raiders? Or how about Madeline Manning-Mims, the Olympic speedster? Or how about Josh Davis, the gold medal-winning Olympic swimmer?

Well, these athletes all have beautiful feet, that's for sure. But in reality, the beauty of their feet has nothing to do with their sports prowess. No, the beauty of their feet comes from this fact: They have used their fame as world-class winners in sports to let others know about Jesus Christ. They have taken the Great Commission seriously and have used their fame to "bring good news" (Romans 10:15) to those who need to know the Savior.

As you walk the Christian life, consider your path and how your feet look to others.

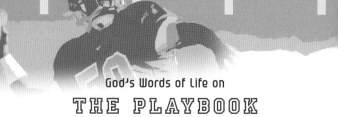

God's Words of Life on

THE PLAYBOOK

Jesus opened their minds so they could understand the Scriptures.

Luke 24:45

How can a young man keep his way pure?
　　By living according to your word.
I seek you with all my heart;
　　do not let me stray from your commands.
I have hidden your word in my heart
　　that I might not sin against you.
Praise be to you, O LORD;
　　teach me your decrees.
With my lips I recount
　　all the laws that come from your mouth.
I rejoice in following your statutes
　　as one rejoices in great riches.
I meditate on your precepts
　　and consider your ways.
I delight in your decrees;
　　I will not neglect your word.

Psalm 119:9–16

The grass withers and the flowers fall,
　　but the word of our God stands forever.

Isaiah 40:8

THE PLAYBOOK

Oh, how I love your law, O LORD!
   I meditate on it all day long.
Your commands make me wiser than my enemies,
   for they are ever with me.
I have more insight than all my teachers,
   for I meditate on your statutes.
I have more understanding than the elders,
   for I obey your precepts.
I have kept my feet from every evil path
   so that I might obey your word.
I have not departed from your laws,
   for you yourself have taught me.
How sweet are your words to my taste,
   sweeter than honey to my mouth!

Psalm 119:97–103

Jesus said, "The Scripture cannot be broken."

John 10:35

We have the word of the prophets made more certain, and you will do well to pay attention to it, as to a light shining in a dark place, until the day dawns and the morning star rises in your hearts.

2 Peter 1:19

God's Words of Life on

THE PLAYBOOK

Your word, O Lord, is eternal;
   it stands firm in the heavens.

Psalm 119:89

*Man does not live on bread alone but on every word
that comes from the mouth of the Lord.*

Deuteronomy 8:3

My eyes stay open through the watches of the night,
   that I may meditate on your promises, O Lord.

Psalm 119:148

*No prophecy of Scripture came about by the prophet's
own interpretation. For prophecy never had its origin in
the will of man, but men spoke from God as they were
carried along by the Holy Spirit.*

2 Peter 1:20–21

Your word, O Lord, is a lamp to my feet
   and a light for my path.

Psalm 119:105

*Do your best to present yourself to God as one
approved, a workman who does not need to be
ashamed and who correctly handles the word of truth.*

2 Timothy 2:15

Devotional Thought on
THE PLAYBOOK

A few years ago, a pro football player made the mistake of his life. He was studying his playbook at a restaurant, and when he got up to leave the restaurant, he forgot it. He left it where others could pick it up, and if they'd had larceny in mind, they could have provided the playbook to an opposing team.

There was one good thing: The player was diligent about studying his playbook. After all, he had taken it with him to the restaurant.

In Joshua's day, the leader of the people didn't have an entire copy of Scripture as we do; he only had the books that Moses had written. But God made it clear that he expected Joshua to study it. In fact, he told Joshua, "Meditate on it day and night, so that you may be careful to do everything written in it" (Joshua 1:8).

Think about the Bible as a playbook. Just as a coach does not write a playbook just to pass the time—he or she wants what is inside to be learned and used—so God gave us his instructions in the Bible so we could read them, think about them, and put them into practice.

Every day. That's how often we are to read this Book God gave us.

Let's strive not to forget the Book.

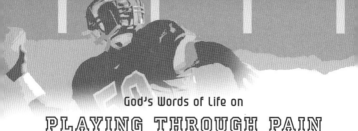

God's Words of Life on

PLAYING THROUGH PAIN

If you suffer for doing good and you endure it, this is commendable before God. To this you were called, because Christ suffered for you, leaving you an example, that you should follow in his steps.

1 Peter 2:20–21

Remember your word to your servant, O Lord,
    for you have given me hope.
My comfort in my suffering is this:
    Your promise preserves my life.

Psalm 119:49–50

Christ was despised and rejected by men,
    a man of sorrows, and familiar with suffering.

Isaiah 53:3

I consider that our present sufferings are not worth comparing with the glory that will be revealed in us.

Romans 8:18

Look upon my suffering and deliver me, O Lord,
    for I have not forgotten your law.
Defend my cause and redeem me;
    preserve my life according to your promise.

Psalm 119:153–154

God's Words of Life on
PLAYING THROUGH PAIN

Do not be surprised at the painful trial you are suffering, as though something strange were happening to you. But rejoice that you participate in the sufferings of Christ, so that you may be overjoyed when his glory is revealed. If you are insulted because of the name of Christ, you are blessed, for the Spirit of glory and of God rests on you…. If you suffer as a Christian, do not be ashamed, but praise God that you bear that name.

1 Peter 4:12–14, 16

Endure hardship with us like a good soldier of Christ Jesus.

2 Timothy 2:3

You, however, know all about my teaching, my way of life, my purpose, faith, patience, love, endurance, persecutions, sufferings—what kinds of things happened to me … the persecutions I endured. Yet the Lord rescued me from all of them.

2 Timothy 3:10–11

The LORD has not despised or disdained
    the suffering of the afflicted one;
he has not hidden his face from him
    but has listened to his cry for help.

Psalm 22:24

This calls for patient endurance and faithfulness on the part of the saints.

Revelation 13:10

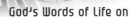

God's Words of Life on

PLAYING THROUGH PAIN

Trials have come so that your faith—of greater worth than gold, which perishes even though refined by fire— may be proved genuine and may result in praise, glory and honor when Jesus Christ is revealed.

1 Peter 1:7

Keep your head in all situations, endure hardship, do the work of an evangelist, discharge all the duties of your ministry.

2 Timothy 4:5

It has been granted to you on behalf of Christ not only to believe on him, but also to suffer for him.

Philippians 1:29

Moses persevered because he saw him who is invisible.

Hebrews 11:27

Remember Jesus Christ, raised from the dead, descended from David. This is my gospel, for which I am suffering even to the point of being chained like a criminal. But God's word is not chained. Therefore I endure everything for the sake of the elect, that they too may obtain the salvation that is in Christ Jesus, with eternal glory.

2 Timothy 2:8–10

Jesus said, "I know your deeds, your hard work and your perseverance.... You have persevered and have endured hardships for my name, and have not grown weary."

Revelation 2:2–3

God's Words of Life on
PLAYING THROUGH PAIN

Praise be to the God and Father of our Lord Jesus Christ, the Father of compassion and the God of all comfort, who comforts us in all our troubles, so that we can comfort those in any trouble with the comfort we ourselves have received from God. For just as the sufferings of Christ flow over into our lives, so also through Christ our comfort overflows.

2 Corinthians 1:3–5

Those who trust in the LORD are like Mount Zion,
    which cannot be shaken but endures forever.
As the mountains surround Jerusalem,
    so the LORD surrounds his people
    both now and forevermore.

Psalm 125:1–2

Let us throw off everything that hinders and the sin that so easily entangles, and let us run with perseverance the race marked out for us. Let us fix our eyes on Jesus, the author and perfecter of our faith, who for the joy set before him endured the cross, scorning its shame, and sat down at the right hand of the throne of God. Consider him who endured such opposition from sinful men, so that you will not grow weary and lose heart.

Hebrews 12:1–3

I want to know Christ and the power of his resurrection and the fellowship of sharing in his sufferings, becoming like him in his death, and so, somehow, to attain to the resurrection from the dead.

Philippians 3:10–11

God's Words of Life on

PLAYING THROUGH PAIN

If we died with Christ,
    we will also live with him;
if we endure,
    we will also reign with him.

2 Timothy 2:11–12

We do not want you to be uninformed, brothers, about the hardships we suffered.... We were under great pressure, far beyond our ability to endure, so that we despaired even of life. Indeed, in our hearts we felt the sentence of death. But this happened that we might not rely on ourselves but on God, who raises the dead. He has delivered us from such a deadly peril, and he will deliver us. On him we have set our hope that he will continue to deliver us, as you help us by your prayers.

2 Corinthians 1:8–11

There was given me a thorn in my flesh, a messenger of Satan, to torment me. Three times I pleaded with the Lord to take it away from me. But he said to me, "My grace is sufficient for you, for my power is made perfect in weakness." Therefore I will boast all the more gladly about my weaknesses, so that Christ's power may rest on me. That is why, for Christ's sake, I delight in weaknesses, in insults, in hardships, in persecutions, in difficulties. For when I am weak, then I am strong.

2 Corinthians 12:7–10

We do not lose heart. Though outwardly we are wasting away, yet inwardly we are being renewed day by day. For our light and momentary troubles are achieving for us an eternal glory that far outweighs them all.

2 Corinthians 4:16–17

Devotional Thought on
PLAYING THROUGH PAIN

Many athletes have turned to faith in Jesus Christ while in the middle of their playing careers. Irving Fryar, Deion Sanders, and Cris Carter all became Christians after their NFL careers were underway. In hoops, there's Hersey Hawkins; in hockey, there's John Vanbiesbrouck.

It was not always easy for these players when they began doing good—when they began their new lives in Christ. Sometimes, they had to suffer because of their efforts. For instance, Gary Gaetti was a member of the Minnesota Twins when he became a believer. Before Gaetti's transformation, he and his buddy Kent Hrbek spent a lot of time together. Much of that time was spent drinking. You'd think fans in Minnesota would appreciate the fact that their star middle infielder was no longer getting drunk and could now concentrate on baseball. On the contrary, they thought Gaetti's new interest in right living made him a soft baseball player, so they and the media began to criticize him. It wasn't long before Gaetti wanted to get out of Minnesota.

Sometimes when we do what is right, we get treated wrong.

Have you suffered for doing what is right? That's great! According to Peter, if that happens, then you are "blessed" (1 Peter 3:14). You are privileged in God's eyes for you have suffered for his name.

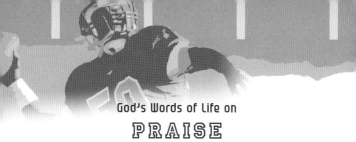

God's Words of Life on

PRAISE

The LORD lives! Praise be to my Rock!
Exalted be God my Savior!

Psalm 18:46

The LORD is my strength and my song;
he has become my salvation.
He is my God, and I will praise him,
my father's God, and I will exalt him.

Exodus 15:2

I will give thanks to the LORD because of his
righteousness
and will sing praise to the name of the LORD Most
High.

Psalm 7:17

I will praise the LORD, who counsels me;
even at night my heart instructs me.
I have set the LORD always before me.
Because he is at my right hand,
I will not be shaken.

Psalm 16:7–8

Great is the LORD, and most worthy of praise,
in the city of our God, his holy mountain.

Psalm 48:1

God's Words of Life on
PRAISE

I will proclaim the name of the LORD.
Oh, praise the greatness of our God!
He is the Rock, his works are perfect,
and all his ways are just.
A faithful God who does no wrong,
upright and just is he.

Deuteronomy 32:3–4

The heavens declare the glory of God;
the skies proclaim the work of his hands.
Day after day they pour forth speech;
night after night they display knowledge.
There is no speech or language
where their voice is not heard.
Their voice goes out into all the earth,
their words to the ends of the world.

Psalm 19:1–4

Sing joyfully to the LORD, you righteous;
it is fitting for the upright to praise him.
Praise the LORD with the harp;
make music to him on the ten-stringed lyre.
Sing to him a new song;
play skillfully, and shout for joy.

Psalm 33:1–2

God's Words of Life on
PRAISE

Sing to the LORD a new song,
for he has done marvelous things;
his right hand and his holy arm
have worked salvation for him.

Psalm 98:1

May the peoples praise you, O God;
may all the peoples praise you.
May the nations be glad and sing for joy,
for you rule the peoples justly
and guide the nations of the earth.

Psalm 67:3–4

*Give glory to the LORD, the God of Israel, and give him
the praise.*

Joshua 7:19

Sing for joy to God our strength;
shout aloud to the God of Jacob!
Begin the music, strike the tambourine,
play the melodious harp and lyre.

Psalm 81:1–2

O LORD, I praise you because I am fearfully and
wonderfully made;
your works are wonderful,
I know that full well.

Psalm 139:14

God's Words of Life on
PRAISE

Praise the LORD, all you nations;
    extol him, all you peoples.
For great is his love toward us,
    and the faithfulness of the LORD endures forever.
Psalm 117:1–2

May my lips overflow with praise, O LORD,
    for you teach me your decrees.
May my tongue sing of your word,
    for all your commands are righteous.
Psalm 119:171–172

*Through Jesus ... let us continually offer to God a sacrifice
of praise—the fruit of lips that confess his name.*
Hebrews 13:15

I will praise you, O LORD, with all my heart....
I will bow down toward your holy temple
    and will praise your name
    for your love and your faithfulness,
for you have exalted above all things
    your name and your word.

Psalm 138:1–2

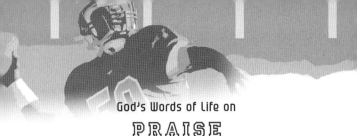

God's Words of Life on
PRAISE

How good it is to sing praises to our God,
how pleasant and fitting to praise him!

Psalm 147:1

Praise the LORD from the earth,
you great sea creatures and all ocean depths,
lightning and hail, snow and clouds,
stormy winds that do his bidding,
you mountains and all hills,
fruit trees and all cedars,
wild animals and all cattle,
small creatures and flying birds,
kings of the earth and all nations,
you princes and all rulers on earth,
young men and maidens,
old men and children.

Psalm 148:7–12

Let everything that has breath praise the Lord.

Psalm 150:6

Praise be to the LORD, the God of Israel,
from everlasting to everlasting.
Let all the people say, "Amen!"

Psalm 106:48

Devotional Thought on
PRAISE

Think back over the years and remember the great athletes who gave glory to God after a win or great accomplishment.

Remember Orel Hershiser winning the World Series and praising God? Think of Michelle Akers, World Cup winner and Olympic gold medalist in soccer, who shares her testimony freely. When Joe Carter won the World Series with a home run, he gave thanks to God. And Jean Driscoll, eight-time winner of the wheelchair Boston Marathon, also boldly shares her faith. In football, Joe Gibbs, coach of the Super Bowl XXVI-winning Washington Redskins, gave glory to God. So did Reggie White, Kurt Warner, and Trent Dilfer after their teams won the Vince Lombardi trophy.

These athletes have learned the vital truth of Psalm 34:1, which says, "I will extol the Lord at all times; his praise will always be on my lips."

But praise is not just for those who take home the championship. Sheila Taormina proved that when she finished sixth in the 2000 Olympic triathlon in Sydney. She continued to praise God despite her disappointment. She demonstrated that praising God is an all-the-time thing—not just a "we-won" thing.

Whether we win a championship or not, we must find ways to "extol the Lord at all times." After all, when all is said and done and God's plans are all revealed, we win! Praise God!

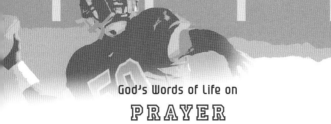

God's Words of Life on

PRAYER

Pray in the Spirit on all occasions with all kinds of prayers and requests. With this in mind, be alert and always keep on praying for all the saints.

Ephesians 6:18

In the morning, O LORD, you hear my voice;
    in the morning I lay my requests before you
    and wait in expectation.

Psalm 5:3

I call on you, O God, for you will answer me;
    give ear to me and hear my prayer.

Psalm 17:6

I pray to you, O LORD,
    in the time of your favor;
in your great love, O God,
    answer me with your sure salvation.

Psalm 69:13

You are forgiving and good, O Lord,
    abounding in love to all who call to you.

Psalm 86:5

God's Words of Life on
PRAYER

....

The LORD our God is near us whenever we pray to him.

Deuteronomy 4:7

O LORD, the God who saves me,
   day and night I cry out before you.
May my prayer come before you;
   turn your ear to my cry.

Psalm 88:1–2

O LORD, hear my prayer,
   listen to my cry for mercy;
in your faithfulness and righteousness
   come to my relief.

Psalm 143:1

"As soon as you began to pray, an answer was given."

Daniel 9:23

Jesus fell with his face to the ground and prayed, "My Father, if it is possible, may this cup be taken from me. Yet not as I will, but as you will."

Matthew 26:39

God's Words of Life on
PRAYER

Devote yourselves to prayer, being watchful and thankful.
Colossians 4:2

The prayer of a righteous man is powerful and effective.
James 5:16

Jesus told his disciples a parable to show them that they should always pray and not give up.
Luke 18:1

The Spirit helps us in our weakness. We do not know what we ought to pray for, but the Spirit himself intercedes for us with groans that words cannot express.
Romans 8:26

Jesus said, "Whatever you ask for in prayer, believe that you have received it, and it will be yours."
Mark 11:24

Be clear minded and self-controlled so that you can pray.
1 Peter 4:7

God's Words of Life on

PRAYER

The prayer of the upright pleases the Lord.

Proverbs 15:8

The LORD has heard my cry for mercy;
   the LORD accepts my prayer.

Psalm 6:9

Hear, O LORD, my righteous plea;
   listen to my cry.
Give ear to my prayer—
   it does not rise from deceitful lips.

Psalm 17:1

O you who hear prayer,
   to you all men will come.

Psalm 65:2

Listen to my prayer, O God,
   do not ignore my plea;
hear me and answer me.

Psalm 55:1–2

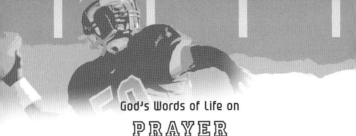

God's Words of Life on

PRAYER

I am a man of prayer.

Psalm 109:4

Hear my prayer, O LORD God Almighty;
listen to me, O God of Jacob.

Psalm 84:8

Have mercy on me, O Lord,
for I call to you all day long.
Bring joy to your servant,
for to you, O Lord,
I lift up my soul.

Psalm 86:3–4

I cry to you for help, O LORD;
in the morning my prayer comes before you.

Psalm 88:13

Be joyful in hope, patient in affliction, faithful in prayer.

Romans 12:12

Devotional Thought on
PRAYER

I've been at the sites of various Super Bowls. I've stood and looked over the field where, for one season at least, the best two football teams in the NFL battled each other for supremacy.

I've also been at the site of what we might call the Super Bowl of prayer. I've looked over the hillside of Mount Carmel, where the reigning religious group in Ahab's day took on a lonely prophet in a great test of prayer supremacy.

I'll take Mount Carmel any day.

On the football field, people have competed for the Lombardi Trophy, and that's pretty cool. But on that grassy hill, God showed a watching nation that he is not to be mocked, that he alone has the power to work miracles, and that idols are hopeless, worthless objects.

On that famous hillside, Elijah's prayer touched God's heart, and God sent fire from heaven. That magnificent manifestation of God's power silenced the prophets of Baal and tuned a hillside full of idol worshipers into men and women who fell to the ground, crying out: "The LORD—he is God!" (1 Kings 18:39).

In our drive to follow our favorite sport, let's never lose sight of the truth that even a thrilling championship game cannot come close to being as exciting as engaging God in a life of prayer.

God's Words of Life on

PRIORITIES

"I am the LORD your God....
You shall have no other gods before me."

Exodus 20:2–3

Let them know that you, whose name is the LORD—
that you alone are the Most High over all the earth.

Psalm 83:18

Jesus said, "Do not worry, saying, 'What shall we eat?'
or 'What shall we drink?' or 'What shall we wear?' For
[unbelievers] run after all these things, and your heavenly
Father knows that you need them. But seek first his
kingdom and his righteousness, and all these things will
be given to you as well."

Matthew 6:31–33

Jesus said, "Whoever wants to save his life will lose it, but
whoever loses his life for me will find it. What good will it
be for a man if he gains the whole world, yet forfeit his
soul? Or what can a man give in exchange for his soul?"

Matthew 16:25–26

Command those who are rich in this present world not
to be arrogant nor to put their hope in wealth, which is
so uncertain, but to put their hope in God, who richly
provides us with everything for our enjoyment.

1 Timothy 6:17

The kingdom of heaven is like treasure hidden in a field. When a man found it, he hid it again, and then in his joy went and sold all he had and bought that field.

Matthew 13:44

An expert in the law ... tested Jesus with this question: "Teacher, which is the greatest commandment in the Law?" Jesus replied: "'Love the Lord your God with all your heart and with all your soul and with all your mind.' This is the first and greatest commandment. And the second is like it: 'Love your neighbor as yourself.' All the Law and the Prophets hang on these two commandments."

Matthew 22:35–40

We fix our eyes not on what is seen, but on what is unseen. For what is seen is temporary, but what is unseen is eternal.

2 Corinthians 4:18

Do not love the world or anything in the world. If anyone loves the world, the love of the Father is not in him. For everything in the world—the cravings of sinful man, the lust of his eyes and the boasting of what he has and does—comes not from the Father but from the world. The world and its desires pass away, but the man who does the will of God lives forever.

1 John 2:15–17

Set your minds on things above, not on earthly things. For you died, and your life is now hidden with Christ in God. When Christ, who is your life, appears, then you also will appear with him in glory.

Colossians 3:2–4

God's Words of Life on

PRIORITIES

Jesus said, "Sell your possessions and give to the poor. Provide purses for yourselves that will not wear out, a treasure in heaven that will not be exhausted, where no thief comes near and no moth destroys. For where your treasure is, there your heart will be also."

Luke 12:33–34

The kingdom of heaven is like a merchant looking for fine pearls. When he found one of great value, he went away and sold everything he had and bought it.

Matthew 13:45-46

Honor the LORD with your wealth,
    with the firstfruits of all your crops;
then your barns will be filled to overflowing,
    and your vats will brim over with new wine.

Proverbs 3:9–10

Jesus went out and saw a tax collector by the name of Levi sitting at his tax booth. "Follow me," Jesus said to him, and Levi got up, left everything and followed him.

Luke 5:27–28

Jesus said, "I am the Alpha and the Omega, the First and the Last, the Beginning and the End."

Revelation 22:13

Devotional Thought on
PRIORITIES

Take it from a two-sport man, something has to have top place in your life.

When Charlie Ward was in college at Florida State University, he was not only a Heisman Trophy-winning football player, but he was also a pretty good basketball player for the Seminoles.

But Charlie Ward knows that although a person may have a couple of different interests, it is important for one thing to have top priority. "It's always good to have Christ in your life first and foremost," he says, "because once you have him first, everything else is something he's blessed you with, something extra."

Here's how Jesus stated that principle in the Sermon on the Mount: "No one can serve two masters. Either he will hate the one and love the other, or he will be devoted to the one and despise the other" (Matthew 6:24). Jesus was specifically talking about God and money in this passage, but the basic principle applies to all of life. In no situation are we to put anything before God. We cannot serve God and something we put before him.

Life is about putting first things first. And that first thing must be God. "Keep things prioritized, and everything will be fine," Charlie Ward reminds us.

That's good advice from a two-sport man who knows how to put first things first in life.

God's Words of Life on

RIGHTEOUSNESS

Blessed are they whose ways are blameless,
   who walk according to the law of the LORD.
Blessed are they who keep his statutes
   and seek him with all their heart.
They do nothing wrong;
   they walk in his ways.

Psalm 119:1–3

*What does the LORD your God ask of you but to fear the
LORD your God, to walk in all his ways, to love him, to
serve the LORD your God with all your heart and with all
your soul, and to observe the LORD's commands and
decrees?*

Deuteronomy 10:12–13

Fear the LORD and serve him with all faithfulness.

Joshua 24:14

*Do what is right and good in the LORD's sight, so that it
may go well with you.*

Deuteronomy 6:18

Commit your way to the LORD;
   trust in him and he will do this:
He will make your righteousness shine like the dawn,
   the justice of your cause like the noonday sun.

Psalm 37:5–6

God's Words of Life on
RIGHTEOUSNESS

In righteousness I will see your face, O LORD;
   when I awake, I will be satisfied with seeing your
   likeness.

Psalm 17:15

The LORD watches over the way of the righteous.

Psalm 1:6

I was young and now I am old,
   yet I have never seen the righteous forsaken
   or their children begging bread.
They are always generous and lend freely;
   their children will be blessed.

Psalm 37:25–26

The LORD has set apart the godly for himself.

Psalm 4:3

The righteousness of the blameless makes a straight
way for them.

Proverbs 11:5

The LORD is my shepherd....
He guides me in paths of righteousness
   for his name's sake.

Psalm 23:1, 3

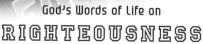

God's Words of Life on

RIGHTEOUSNESS

The LORD has dealt with me according to my
    righteousness;
    according to the cleanness of my hands he has
        rewarded me.
For I have kept the ways of the LORD;
    I have not done evil by turning from my God.
All his laws are before me;
    I have not turned away from his decrees.

Psalm 18:20–22

Who may ascend the hill of the LORD?
    Who may stand in his holy place?
He who has clean hands and a pure heart,
    who does not lift up his soul to an idol
    or swear by what is false.
He will receive blessing from the LORD
    and vindication from God his Savior.

Psalm 24:3–5

The eyes of the LORD are on the righteous
    and his ears are attentive to their cry.

Psalm 34:15

*God's divine power has given us everything we need
for life and godliness through our knowledge of him
who called us by his own glory and goodness.*

2 Peter 1:3

God's Words of Life on

RIGHTEOUSNESS

The righteous will flourish like a palm tree,
   they will grow like a cedar of Lebanon;
planted in the house of the LORD,
   they will flourish in the courts of our God.

Psalm 92:12–13

Whoever of you loves life
   and desires to see many good days,
keep your tongue from evil
   and your lips from speaking lies.
Turn from evil and do good;
   seek peace and pursue it.

Psalm 34:12–14

*You were once darkness, but now you are light in the
Lord. Live as children of light (for the fruit of the light
consists in all goodness, righteousness and truth) and
find out what pleases the Lord.*

Ephesians 5:8–10

Trust in the LORD and do good;
   dwell in the land and enjoy safe pasture.
Delight yourself in the LORD
   and he will give you the desires of your heart.

Psalm 37:3–4

God's Words of Life on

RIGHTEOUSNESS

Lead me, O Lord, in your righteousness ...
    make straight your way before me.

Psalm 5:8

Blessed is the man who fears the Lord,
    who finds great delight in his commands.
His children will be mighty in the land;
    the generation of the upright will be blessed.
Wealth and riches are in his house,
    and his righteousness endures forever.
Even in darkness light dawns for the upright,
    for the gracious and compassionate and righteous
        man.
Good will come to him who is generous and lends
        freely,
    who conducts his affairs with justice.
Surely he will never be shaken;
    a righteous man will be remembered forever.
He will have no fear of bad news;
    his heart is steadfast, trusting in the Lord.
His heart is secure, he will have no fear;
    in the end he will look in triumph on his foes.
He has scattered abroad his gifts to the poor,
    his righteousness endures forever.

Psalm 112:1–9

Devotional Thought on
RIGHTEOUSNESS

Let's see if we can find athletes who characterize the traits of a righteous person as detailed in Psalm 112.

He "fears the LORD" (verse 1). In 1995 Danny Wuerffel was one of the best college football players in the land. A pornographic magazine wanted to name him to its All-American team. Wuerffel turned it down. He knew that God's principles for right living are not to be trifled with.

"Even in darkness light dawns" (verse 4). Andre Ware was a high school basketball player—a Christian. When he was injured in a freak accident during practice, he lost the use of his legs. Yet he continued to trust God.

"His heart is secure, he will have no fear" (verse 8). A. C. Green steadfastly refused to give in to the pressures of a promiscuous era, all the while setting the record for most consecutive games played in the NBA.

"He has scattered abroad his gifts to the poor" (verse 9). Betsy King, Hall of Fame golfer, has set the standard for helping others with her work with the poor in Tanzania.

Righteous people like these athletes have set the example for us. Their examples can encourage us to strive harder and to depend more completely on the Holy Spirit to help us be the kind of righteous person described in Psalm 112.

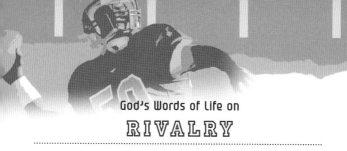

God's Words of Life on
RIVALRY

To you, O LORD, I lift up my soul;
    in you I trust, O my God.
Do not let me be put to shame,
    nor let my enemies triumph over me.
No one whose hope is in you
    will ever be put to shame.

Psalm 25:1–3

Jesus told his disciples, "If the world hates you, keep in mind that it hated me first. If you belonged to the world, it would love you as its own. As it is, you do not belong to the world, but I have chosen you out of the world. That is why the world hates you. Remember the words I spoke to you: 'No servant is greater than his master.' If they persecuted me, they will persecute you also."

John 15:18–20

We were harassed at every turn—conflicts on the outside, fears within. But God, who comforts the downcast, comforted us.

2 Corinthians 7:5

Jesus said, "If people do not welcome you, shake the dust off your feet when you leave their town, as a testimony against them."

Luke 9:5

God's Words of Life on
RIVALRY

For your name's sake, O LORD, preserve my life;
in your righteousness, bring me out of trouble.
In your unfailing love, silence my enemies ...
for I am your servant.

Psalm 143:11–12

*We are hard pressed on every side, but not crushed;
perplexed, but not in despair; persecuted, but not
abandoned; struck down, but not destroyed.*

2 Corinthians 4:8–9

*Do not take revenge, my friends, but leave room for
God's wrath, for it is written: "It is mine to avenge; I will
repay," says the Lord.*

Romans 12:19

*Whatever happens, conduct yourselves in a manner
worthy of the gospel of Christ. Then, whether I come
and see you or only hear about you in my absence, I will
know that you stand firm in one spirit, contending as one
man for the faith of the gospel without being frightened
in any way by those who oppose you.*

Philippians 1:27–28

*The Lord's servant must not quarrel; instead, he must
be kind to everyone, able to teach, not resentful. Those
who oppose him he must gently instruct, in the hope
that God will grant them repentance leading them to a
knowledge of the truth.*

2 Timothy 2:24–25

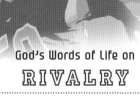

God's Words of Life on
RIVALRY

Though I walk in the midst of trouble, O LORD,
  you preserve my life;
you stretch out your hand against the anger of my foes,
  with your right hand you save me.

Psalm 138:7

*An overseer must hold firmly to the trustworthy message
as it has been taught, so that he can encourage others by
sound doctrine and refute those who oppose it.*

Titus 1:9

O Lord, you took up my case;
  you redeemed my life.
You have seen, O LORD, the wrong done to me.
  Uphold my cause!

Lamentations 3:58–59

*In everything set them an example by doing what is
good. In your teaching show integrity, seriousness and
soundness of speech that cannot be condemned, so
that those who oppose you may be ashamed because
they have nothing bad to say about us.*

Titus 2:7–8

*Jesus said, "I will give you words and wisdom that none
of your adversaries will be able to resist or contradict."*

Luke 21:15

Devotional Thought on
RIVALRY

Ohio State and Michigan in college football. Connecticut and Tennessee in women's college hoops. Russia and the United States in gymnastics. The Dodgers and the Giants in baseball. These teams have, over the years, formed bitter rivalries.

Usually, though, the rivalries play themselves out in harmless ways. The teams pound each other for a couple of hours, fans yell themselves hoarse, and somebody wins temporary bragging rights. Generally, it's all in good fun.

But the Cain and Abel rivalry (Genesis 4) was no Nebraska-Oklahoma football rivalry. Theirs was real hatred accompanied by jealousy at its worst.

The real basis of their rivalry lay in the difference they saw in their relationships with God. Isn't that the way it often is? Cain was not willing to present the kind of offering God required, and when Abel did, trouble erupted.

Cain hated Abel because Abel was righteous.

You'll run into that a lot in life. Those who do not like your faith or the fact that you have a reverence for God will become your instant rivals. And while they may not take the Cain approach and attempt to do you physical harm, they can be troublesome.

The best way to handle a Cain-sized problem is to trust God and continue to do what is right. We can't let a rivalry turn us away from God's guidance and help.

God's Words of Life on

THE RULES

If anyone competes as an athlete, he does not receive the victor's crown unless he competes according to the rules.

2 Timothy 2:5

He has showed you, O man, what is good.
　　And what does the LORD require of you?
To act justly and to love mercy
　　and to walk humbly with your God.

Micah 6:8

Great peace have they who love your law,
　　and nothing can make them stumble.
I wait for your salvation, O LORD,
　　and I follow your commands.
I obey your statutes,
　　for I love them greatly.
I obey your precepts and your statutes,
　　for all my ways are known to you.

Psalm 119:165–168

Whoever practices and teaches these commands will be called great in the kingdom of heaven.

Matthew 5:19

God's Words of Life on

THE RULES

Take to heart all the words I have solemnly declared to you this day, so that you may command your children to obey carefully all the words of this law. They are not just idle words for you—they are your life.

Deuteronomy 32:46–47

Love the LORD your God and keep his requirements, his decrees, his laws and his commands always.

Deuteronomy 11:1

Do not merely listen to the word, and so deceive yourselves. Do what it says.

James 1:22

Jesus said, "Whoever has my commands and obeys them, he is the one who loves me. He who loves me will be loved by my Father, and I too will love him and show myself to him."

John 14:21

These commands are a lamp,
   this teaching is a light,
and the corrections of discipline
   are the way to life.

Proverbs 6:23

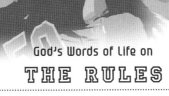

God's Words of Life on

THE RULES

*"The most important [commandment]," answered Jesus,
"is this: 'Hear, O Israel, the Lord our God, the Lord is one.
Love the Lord your God with all your heart and with all
your soul and with all your mind and with all your
strength.' The second is this: 'Love your neighbor as
yourself.' There is no commandment greater than these."*

Mark 12:29–31

This is love for God: to obey his commands.

1 John 5:3

All your commands are trustworthy, O LORD.

Psalm 119:86

I desire to do your will, O my God;
   your law is within my heart.

Psalm 40:8

O LORD, your commands are my delight.

Psalm 119:143

*If you really keep the royal law found in Scripture, "Love
your neighbor as yourself," you are doing right.*

James 2:8

God's Words of Life on
THE RULES

When Gentiles, who do not have the law, do by nature things required by the law, they are a law for themselves, even though they do not have the law, since they show that the requirements of the law are written on their hearts, their consciences also bearing witness.

Romans 2:14–15

To all perfection I see a limit;
　　but your commands, O Lord, are boundless.

Psalm 119:96

I run in the path of your commands, O Lord,
　　for you have set my heart free.

Psalm 119:32

"I will put my law in their minds
　　and write it on their hearts.
I will be their God,
　　and they will be my people,"
　　　　declares the Lord.

Jeremiah 31:33

God's Words of Life on

THE RULES

The law of the LORD is perfect,
   reviving the soul.
The statutes of the LORD are trustworthy,
   making wise the simple.
The precepts of the LORD are right,
   giving joy to the heart.
The commands of the LORD are radiant,
   giving light to the eyes.
The fear of the LORD is pure,
   enduring forever.
The ordinances of the LORD are sure
   and altogether righteous.
They are more precious than gold,
   than much pure gold;
they are sweeter than honey,
   than honey from the comb.
By them is your servant warned;
   in keeping them there is great reward.

Psalm 19:7–11

*I have fought the good fight, I have finished the race, I
have kept the faith. Now there is in store for me the
crown of righteousness, which the Lord, the righteous
Judge, will award to me on that day—and not only to
me, but also to all who have longed for his appearing.*

2 Timothy 4:7–8

Devotional Thought on
THE RULES

Have the Ten Commandments fallen on hard times? They can't be displayed in schools, and many people can't name them.

Bobby Bowden, the venerable longtime coach of Florida State football, commented a few years ago on the problem. He said, "So many kids now that I'm coaching that are coming up, they think no more of breaking the law than the man in the moon. Some of them don't even know the Ten Commandments. I sure appreciate my parents disciplining me and trying to teach me what was right."

Many young people have been brought up without knowing the Ten Commandments, but that does not give them—or us—a reason to ignore God's commands.

A missionary to Indonesia was translating Scripture into the language of the people. As she did her work, she wondered if they would be able to comprehend the difference between right and wrong. So she asked the people to begin naming what they felt were the top rules for living. To her shock, these people, who had never even heard of the Bible, named the rules that we know as the Ten Commandments.

When God codified those rules and etched them in stone for Moses, he was not making up new rules. He was simply putting down in writing what he had already put in every human heart.

SIGNIFICANCE

Jesus said, "Are not five sparrows sold for two pennies? Yet not one of them is forgotten by God. Indeed, the very hairs of your head are all numbered. Don't be afraid; you are worth more than many sparrows."

Luke 12:6–7

Jesus said, "If a man owns a hundred sheep, and one of them wanders away, will he not leave the ninety-nine on the hills and go to look for the one that wandered off? And if he finds it, I tell you the truth, he is happier about that one sheep than about the ninety-nine that did not wander off."

Matthew 18:12–13

Jesus said, "See how the lilies of the field grow. They do not labor or spin. Yet I tell you that not even Solomon in all his splendor was dressed like one of these. If that is how God clothes the grass of the field, which is here today and tomorrow is thrown into the fire, will he not much more clothe you?"

Matthew 6:28–30

Jesus said, "Suppose a woman has ten silver coins and loses one. Does she not light a lamp, sweep the house and search carefully until she finds it? And when she finds it, she calls her friends and neighbors together and says, 'Rejoice with me; I have found my lost coin.' In the same way, I tell you, there is rejoicing in the presence of the angels of God over one sinner who repents."

Luke 15:8–10

God's Words of Life on
SIGNIFICANCE

Jesus said, "Let the little children come to me, and do not hinder them, for the kingdom of heaven belongs to such as these."

Matthew 19:14

The LORD tends his flock like a shepherd:
 He gathers the lambs in his arms
and carries them close to his heart;
  he gently leads those that have young.

Isaiah 40:11

Jesus said, "Whatever you did for one of the least of these brothers of mine, you did for me."

Matthew 25:40

Jesus saw the rich putting their gifts into the temple treasury. He also saw a poor widow put in two very small copper coins. "I tell you the truth," he said, "this poor widow has put in more than all the others. All these people gave their gifts out of their wealth; but she out of her poverty put in all she had to live on."

Luke 21:1–4

A woman came to Jesus with an alabaster jar of very expensive perfume, which she poured on his head as he was reclining at the table. When the disciples saw this, they were indignant.... Jesus said to them, "Why are you bothering this woman? She has done a beautiful thing to me.... Wherever this gospel is preached throughout the world, what she has done will also be told, in memory of her."

Matthew 26:7–8, 10, 13

From now on we regard no one from a worldly point of view. Though we once regarded Christ in this way, we do so no longer. Therefore, if anyone is in Christ, he is a new creation; the old has gone, the new has come!

2 Corinthians 5:16–17

Jesus said, "To him who overcomes, I will ... give him a white stone with a new name written on it, known only to him who receives it."

Revelation 2:17

As Jesus walked beside the Sea of Galilee, he saw Simon and his brother Andrew casting a net into the lake, for they were fishermen. "Come, follow me," Jesus said, "and I will make you fishers of men."

Mark 1:16–17

Jesus said, "Him who overcomes I will ... write on him the name of my God and the name of the city of my God, the new Jerusalem, which is coming down out of heaven from my God; and I will also write on him my new name."

Revelation 3:12

Jesus asked his disciples, "Who do you say I am?" Simon Peter answered, "You are the Christ, the Son of the living God." Jesus replied, "Blessed are you, Simon son of Jonah, for this was not revealed to you by man, but by my Father in heaven. And I tell you that you are Peter, and on this rock I will build my church."

Matthew 16:15–18

Devotional Thought on
SIGNIFICANCE

Sometimes sports stories have funny names in them. Sure, sports has Marion Jones, Dan Marino, Drew Henson, Betsy King, and Bobby Hull. Those are common names.

But sports also has Van Lingo Mungo (baseball), Picabo Street (Olympic skier), and Ickey Woods (football).

Yet as odd sounding as some of those names might be to us, they are significant in sports because it's important to make sure everyone is mentioned. No contribution to sports is too small to be remembered.

In the Bible we also read many common names: Abraham, Deborah, Esther, Daniel, Ruth, and Paul.

But the Bible also has names like Adonikam, Bigvai, Azmaveth, Nebo, Lod, and Zattu (Ezra 2). Insignificant? Not at all. These were leaders of groups of people who came back from Babylon. Their part in the biblical record is indeed small, but they were important enough for God to mention.

There is more than one reason for that. First, these people had key roles. Second—and this is the good news for us—every name is significant to God.

Sometimes in this fame-is-everything world, we can easily think that because we might not have a recognizable name or we don't get much notice, we lack worth. That's not true. God cares. He loves everyone just the same.

That's great news—no matter what our name is.

God's Words of Life on
TEAMMATES

Two are better than one,
   because they have a good return for their work:
If one falls down,
   his friend can help him up.
But pity the man who falls
   and has no one to help him up!...
Though one may be overpowered,
   two can defend themselves.
A cord of three strands is not quickly broken.

Ecclesiastes 4:9–10, 12

Let us not give up meeting together, as some are in the habit of doing, but let us encourage one another—and all the more as you see the Day approaching.

Hebrews 10:25

We sent Timothy, who is our brother and God's fellow worker in spreading the gospel of Christ, to strengthen and encourage you in your faith.

1 Thessalonians 3:2

Let the word of Christ dwell in you richly as you teach and admonish one another with all wisdom, and as you sing psalms, hymns and spiritual songs with gratitude in your hearts to God.

Colossians 3:16

God's Words of Life on
TEAMMATES

As iron sharpens iron,
so one man sharpens another.

Proverbs 27:17

Confess your sins to each other and pray for each other.
James 5:16

I myself am convinced, my brothers, that you your-selves are full of goodness, complete in knowledge and competent to instruct one another.
Romans 15:14

Encourage one another daily, as long as it is called Today.
Hebrews 3:13

Be devoted to one another in brotherly love.
Romans 12:10

Judas and Silas, who themselves were prophets, said much to encourage and strengthen the brothers.
Acts 15:32

A friend loves at all times,
and a brother is born for adversity.

Proverbs 17:17

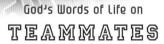

God's Words of Life on

TEAMMATES

He who walks with the wise grows wise.

Proverbs 13:20

Jesus said, "If two of you on earth agree about anything you ask for, it will be done for you by my Father in heaven. For where two or three come together in my name, there am I with them."

Matthew 18:19–20

Epaphras, who is one of you and a servant of Christ Jesus, sends greetings. He is always wrestling in prayer for you, that you may stand firm in all the will of God, mature and fully assured.

Colossians 4:12

Encourage one another and build each other up, just as in fact you are doing.

1 Thessalonians 5:11

Joshua fought the Amalekites as Moses had ordered, and Moses, Aaron and Hur went to the top of the hill. As long as Moses held up his hands, the Israelites were winning, but whenever he lowered his hands, the Amalekites were winning. When Moses' hands grew tired, they took a stone and put it under him and he sat on it. Aaron and Hur held his hands up—one on one side, one on the other—so that his hands remained steady.

Exodus 17:10–12

Jesus said, "Strengthen your brothers."

Luke 22:32

Devotional Thought on
TEAMMATES

One of the neatest pro football stories I've heard involves three talented members of the Buffalo Bills.

It all began a few years ago when tight end Jay Riemersma joined the Bills after being drafted out of the University of Michigan. When he arrived in Buffalo, he was soon befriended by All-Pro defensive lineman Bryce Paup. Both players were Christians, so Paup devised a plan. When Riemersma was on the field on offense, Paup would pray for him; and when Paup was on the field on defense, Jay would pray for him.

They decided that they would be good company for each other and that they would lift each other up. They would challenge and encourage each other, helping each become a better Christian.

When Paup left Buffalo to play for another team, Riemersma sought another prayer partner, and he found Kenny Irvin. Soon they were exchanging sideline prayer times during Bills games.

These players proved the inverse of the frightening truth of 1 Corinthians 15:33, which says, "Bad company corrupts good character." They decided to find good company so their character could be improved rather than corrupted.

Running back Shaun Alexander, who was drafted by the Seattle Seahawks after a fine college career, put it like this: "You've just got to surround yourself with other people who have the same goals."

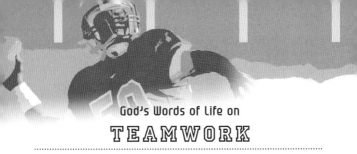

God's Words of Life on
TEAMWORK

Just as each of us has one body with many members, and these members do not all have the same function, so in Christ we who are many form one body, and each member belongs to all the others. We have different gifts, according to the grace given us.

Romans 12:4–6

In the church God has appointed first of all apostles, second prophets, third teachers, then workers of miracles, also those having gifts of healing, those able to help others, those with gifts of administration, and those speaking in different kinds of tongues. Are all apostles? Are all prophets? Are all teachers? Do all work miracles? Do all have gifts of healing? Do all speak in tongues? Do all interpret? But eagerly desire the greater gifts.

1 Corinthians 12:28–31

Since you are eager to have spiritual gifts, try to excel in gifts that build up the church.

1 Corinthians 14:12

Serve one another in love.

Galatians 5:13

Do not neglect your gift.

1 Timothy 4:14

God's Words of Life on
TEAMWORK

Each one should use whatever gift he has received to serve others, faithfully administering God's grace in its various forms. If anyone speaks, he should do it as one speaking the very words of God. If anyone serves, he should do it with the strength God provides, so that in all things God may be praised through Jesus Christ.

1 Peter 4:10–11

Fan into flame the gift of God, which is in you.

2 Timothy 1:6

As we have opportunity, let us do good to all people, especially to those who belong to the family of believers.

Galatians 6:10

Let us therefore make every effort to do what leads to peace and to mutual edification.

Romans 14:19

The Lord has assigned to each his task. I planted the seed, Apollos watered it, but God made it grow. So neither he who plants nor he who waters is anything, but only God, who makes things grow. The man who plants and the man who waters have one purpose, and each will be rewarded according to his own labor. For we are God's fellow workers.

1 Corinthians 3:5–9

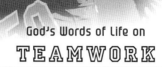

God's Words of Life on

TEAMWORK

Each of you must put off falsehood and speak truthfully to his neighbor, for we are all members of one body.

Ephesians 4:25

There is one body and one Spirit—just as you were called to one hope when you were called—one Lord, one faith, one baptism; one God and Father of all, who is over all and through all and in all. But to each one of us grace has been given as Christ apportioned it. This is why it says:
"When he ascended on high,
he led captives in his train
and gave gifts to men."

Ephesians 4:4–8

They devoted themselves to the apostles' teaching and to the fellowship, to the breaking of bread and to prayer. Everyone was filled with awe, and many wonders and miraculous signs were done by the apostles. All the believers were together and had everything in common. Selling their possessions and goods, they gave to anyone as he had need. Every day they continued to meet together in the temple courts. They broke bread in their homes and ate together with glad and sincere hearts, praising God and enjoying the favor of all the people. And the Lord added to their number daily those who were being saved.

Acts 2:42–47

Devotional Thought on

TEAMWORK

The toughest job of a youth league coach is to convince the eager players that they can't all be the pitcher or the quarterback or the goalie. The high-profile positions seem to draw everyone's interest. However, football can't be played with 11 QBs.

And the work of the church can't be accomplished if everyone is the pastor or the deacon or the teacher. According to Paul, God designed his team members to have specific skills. "It was [Christ] who gave some to be apostles, some to be prophets, some to be evangelists, and some to be pastors and teachers" (Ephesians 4:11). Although the people who hold these jobs in the church do different things, they have the same goal: to build up the body of believers until they "reach unity in the faith and in the knowledge of the Son of God" (verse 13).

These jobs are diverse positions with differing functions, but the people who hold them all work toward the same thing. It sounds like a description of very successful sports teams, such as the powerful Chicago Bulls of the Michael Jordan-Scottie Pippen era.

When the people on a sports team stick to their jobs and do them well, things happen—good things. And the same is true in a church.

God's Words of Life on

TOMORROW'S GAME

"I know the plans I have for you," declares the LORD, "plans to prosper you and not to harm you, plans to give you hope and a future."

Jeremiah 29:11

Jesus said, "Do not worry about tomorrow, for tomorrow will worry about itself."

Matthew 6:34

God has said,
"Never will I leave you;
never will I forsake you."

Hebrews 13:5

Not one of all the good promises the LORD your God gave you has failed. Every promise has been fulfilled; not one has failed.

Joshua 23:14

May the God of hope fill you with all joy and peace as you trust in him, so that you may overflow with hope by the power of the Holy Spirit.

Romans 15:13

Blessed is he who trusts in the LORD.

Proverbs 16:20

TOMORROW'S GAME

Praise be to the God and Father of our Lord Jesus Christ! In his great mercy he has given us new birth into a living hope through the resurrection of Jesus Christ from the dead, and into an inheritance that can never perish, spoil or fade—kept in heaven for you.

1 Peter 1:3–4

Jesus said, "Do not let your hearts be troubled. Trust in God; trust also in me. In my Father's house are many rooms; if it were not so, I would have told you. I am going there to prepare a place for you. And if I go and prepare a place for you, I will come back and take you to be with me that you also may be where I am."

John 14:1–3

On my bed I remember you, O LORD;
    I think of you through the watches of the night.
Because you are my help,
    I sing in the shadow of your wings.
My soul clings to you;
    your right hand upholds me.

Psalm 63:6–8

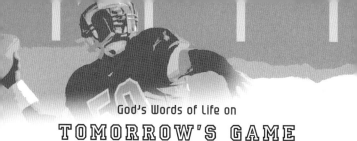

God's Words of Life on

TOMORROW'S GAME

Live holy and godly lives as you look forward to the day of God and speed its coming.... In keeping with his promise we are looking forward to a new heaven and a new earth, the home of righteousness.

2 Peter 3:11–13

Because of the LORD's great love we are not consumed,
  for his compassions never fail.
They are new every morning;
  great is your faithfulness, O LORD.

Lamentations 3:22–23

Blessed is he whose help is the God of Jacob,
  whose hope is in the LORD his God,
the Maker of heaven and earth,
  the sea, and everything in them—
  the LORD, who remains faithful forever.

Psalm 146:5–6

Satisfy us in the morning with your unfailing love,
  O LORD,
  that we may sing for joy and be glad all our days.

Psalm 90:14

Your throne, O God, will last for ever and ever,
  and righteousness will be the scepter of your
    kingdom.

Hebrews 1:8

God's Words of Life on
TOMORROW'S GAME

Faith is being sure of what we hope for and certain of what we do not see.

Hebrews 11:1

Where can I go from your Spirit?
Where can I flee from your presence?
If I go up to the heavens, you are there;
if I make my bed in the depths, you are there.
If I rise on the wings of the dawn,
if I settle on the far side of the sea,
even there your hand will guide me,
your right hand will hold me fast.

Psalm 139:7–10

"I the LORD do not change," declares the LORD.

Malachi 3:6

Trust in the LORD at all times, O people;
pour out your hearts to him,
for God is our refuge.

Psalm 62:8

Because Jesus lives forever, he has a permanent priest-hood. Therefore he is able to save completely those who come to God through him, because he always lives to intercede for them.

Hebrews 7:24–25

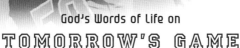

God's Words of Life on

TOMORROW'S GAME

We have this hope as an anchor for the soul, firm and secure.

Hebrews 6:19

Jesus Christ is the same yesterday and today and forever.

Hebrews 13:8

The Lord will rescue me from every evil attack and will bring me safely to his heavenly kingdom.

2 Timothy 4:18

Now we see but a poor reflection as in a mirror; then we shall see face to face. Now I know in part; then I shall know fully, even as I am fully known.

1 Corinthians 13:12

Dear friends, now we are children of God, and what we will be has not yet been made known. But we know that when he appears, we shall be like him, for we shall see him as he is. Everyone who has this hope in him purifies himself, just as he is pure.

1 John 3:2–3

Let the morning bring me word of your unfailing
    love, O Lord,
  for I have put my trust in you.
Show me the way I should go,
  for to you I lift up my soul.

Psalm 143:8

Devotional Thought on
TOMORROW'S GAME

There is nothing sillier than an athlete who guarantees that his or her team is going to win the big game. Even though sometimes those pregame prognostications are right—most notably the accurate 1969 prediction by Joe Namath that his New York Jets from the upstart AFL would beat the Baltimore Colts from the established, ruling NFL—those pregame claims to fame are useless.

No one knows what will happen after the puck is dropped or the ball is kicked off.

Life is more interesting because of its unpredictability and mysteries. God, who knows the history of the world from beginning to end and who knows our life story before it even begins (see Psalm 139), is the only one who knows what will happen tomorrow. In sports or in life, nobody else knows.

So what does that mean for us? First, it means that we should be careful about suggesting that we know what tomorrow will bring. Second, it means that we must leave everything in God's capable, omnipotent hands.

We can't guarantee victories for tomorrow, and we can't predict losses for the next day. What we can do is turn each day over to our Sovereign Lord as it comes, trusting completely in his plans for us.

Come to think of it, that's a pretty victorious way to look at tomorrow.

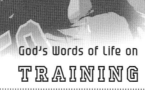

God's Words of Life on

TRAINING

Come, let us go up to the mountain of the LORD,
   to the house of the God of Jacob.
He will teach us his ways,
   so that we may walk in his paths.

Isaiah 2:3

*May the Lord direct your hearts into God's love and
Christ's perseverance.*

2 Thessalonians 3:5

*Jesus said, "When he, the Spirit of truth, comes, he will
guide you into all truth."*

John 16:13

*Jesus went down to Capernaum, a town in Galilee, and
on the Sabbath began to teach the people. They were
amazed at his teaching, because his message had
authority.*

Luke 4:31–32

*Jesus said, "The Counselor, the Holy Spirit, whom the
Father will send in my name, will teach you all things
and will remind you of everything I have said to you."*

John 14:26

Direct my footsteps according to your word, O LORD;
   let no sin rule over me....
Make your face shine upon your servant
   and teach me your decrees.

Psalm 119:133, 135

God's Words of Life on
TRAINING

Teach me, O LORD, to follow your decrees;
　　then I will keep them to the end.
Give me understanding, and I will keep your law
　　and obey it with all my heart.
Direct me in the path of your commands,
　　for there I find delight.
Turn my heart toward your statutes, O LORD,
　　and not toward selfish gain.
Turn my eyes away from worthless things;
　　preserve my life according to your word.

Psalm 119:33–37

Blessed is the man you discipline, O LORD,
　　the man you teach from your law.

Psalm 94:12

Do not make light of the Lord's discipline,
　　and do not lose heart when he rebukes you,
because the Lord disciplines those he loves,
　　and he punishes everyone he accepts as a son.

Hebrews 12:5–6

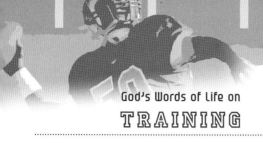

God's Words of Life on

TRAINING

Show me your ways, O LORD,
    teach me your paths;
guide me in your truth and teach me,
    for you are God my Savior,
    and my hope is in you all day long.

Psalm 25:4–5

Jesus said, "Those whom I love I rebuke and discipline."
Revelation 3:19

Let us leave the elementary teachings about Christ and go on to maturity.
Hebrews 6:1

Endure hardship as discipline; God is treating you as sons. For what son is not disciplined by his father? If you are not disciplined (and everyone undergoes discipline), then you are illegitimate children and not true sons. Moreover, we have all had human fathers who disciplined us and we respected them for it. How much more should we submit to the Father of our spirits and live! Our fathers disciplined us for a little while as they thought best; but God disciplines us for our good, that we may share in his holiness. No discipline seems pleasant at the time, but painful. Later on, however, it produces a harvest of righteousness and peace for those who have been trained by it.
Hebrews 12:7–11

Devotional Thought on
TRAINING

. . . .

When he was coach at the University of Nebraska, Tom Osborne made sure his players knew what the game plan for the week was. Early in his career, he had a quarterback who kept throwing interceptions on passes that were clearly not thrown according to the plan. So at that point, Osborne began testing the players on where they were to go and what they were to do in various situations.

Repetition is a great form of teaching, and testing prompts athletes and students alike to repeat information until they can recall it. We may not be too fond of going over information a second time, but repetition is an old, tried-and-true teaching device for a reason. It works.

Moses used it too. In Deuteronomy 14, he reiterated to the people some rules about clean and unclean food—rules that were first recorded in Leviticus 11.

As God looked over his people, he wanted something from them that they knew little about, and right eating would help them achieve that goal. The goal? Holiness.

Our God deeply desires for us to live in a way that prevents harm—both to ourselves and to others.

He doesn't just tell us once; he tells us many times. And then there's the test. Not a written test but a take-home test—an exam lived out in real life.

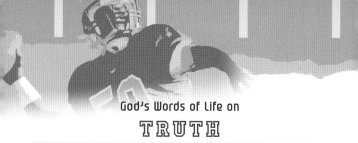

God's Words of Life on
TRUTH

Jesus said, "I tell you the truth."

Matthew 5:26

You also were included in Christ when you heard the word of truth, the gospel of your salvation.

Ephesians 1:13

This is what we speak, not in words taught us by human wisdom but in words taught by the Spirit, expressing spiritual truths in spiritual words.

1 Corinthians 2:13

Jesus said, "Watch out for false prophets. They come to you in sheep's clothing, but inwardly they are ferocious wolves. By their fruit you will recognize them. Do people pick grapes from thornbushes, or figs from thistles? Likewise every good tree bears good fruit, but a bad tree bears bad fruit. A good tree cannot bear bad fruit, and a bad tree cannot bear good fruit. Every tree that does not bear good fruit is cut down and thrown into the fire. Thus, by their fruit you will recognize them."

Matthew 7:15–20

Some false brothers had infiltrated our ranks to spy on the freedom we have in Christ Jesus and to make us slaves. We did not give in to them for a moment, so that the truth of the gospel might remain with you.

Galatians 2:4

God's Words of Life on

TRUTH

They exchanged the truth of God for a lie, and worshiped and served created things rather than the Creator—who is forever praised.

Romans 1:25

Satan himself masquerades as an angel of light. It is not surprising, then, if his servants masquerade as servants of righteousness.

2 Corinthians 11:14–15

You must no longer live as the Gentiles do, in the futility of their thinking. They are darkened in their under-standing and separated from the life of God because of the ignorance that is in them due to the hardening of their hearts. Having lost all sensitivity, they have given themselves over to sensuality so as to indulge in every kind of impurity, with a continual lust for more. You, however, did not come to know Christ that way. Surely you heard of him and were taught in him in accordance with the truth that is in Jesus.

Ephesians 4:17–21

We ought always to thank God for you, brothers loved by the Lord, because from the beginning God chose you to be saved through the sanctifying work of the Spirit and through belief in the truth.

2 Thessalonians 2:13

God our Savior ... wants all men to be saved and to come to a knowledge of the truth.

1 Timothy 2:3–4

God's Words of Life on

TRUTH

....

Don't be deceived, my dear brothers. Every good and perfect gift is from above, coming down from the Father of the heavenly lights, who does not change like shifting shadows. He chose to give us birth through the word of truth, that we might be a kind of firstfruits of all he created.

James 1:16–18

You have an anointing from the Holy One, and all of you know the truth.

1 John 2:20

We are from God, and whoever knows God listens to us; but whoever is not from God does not listen to us. This is how we recognize the Spirit of truth and the spirit of falsehood.

1 John 4:6

It is the Spirit who testifies, because the Spirit is the truth.

1 John 5:6

Jesus said, "I am the way and the truth and the life."

John 14:6

Devotional Thought on
TRUTH

In sports, if you can legally get away with a trick play, then you have every right to try it.

The most famous trick play in pro football was used by the Tennessee Titans to save themselves from playoff elimination in 1999. They pulled off an incredible lateral play on a kick return—a play that looked like a forward pass but wasn't one.

Then, of course, there are the old standards, such as the fake punt. These tricks work because they deceive the other team into thinking one thing is going to happen when the team in control knows something else is going to happen.

But what is merely fun and games in sports is serious business in the spiritual realm. Our God cares deeply that we not get fooled by tricksters who say one thing—which might sound as though it comes from God—but mean something totally different. Paul said, "See to it that no one takes you captive through hollow and deceptive philosophy, which depends on human tradition and the basic principles of this world rather than on Christ" (Colossians 2:8).

We can be snared by worldly or even demonic philosophies if we are not firmly grounded in God's truth. Before God, let us examine our thinking to ensure that it is based on God's truth and is presented in his way.

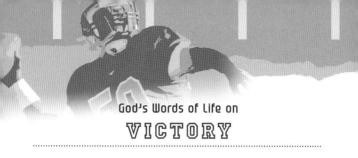

God's Words of Life on

VICTORY

It is God who arms me with strength
   and makes my way perfect.
He makes my feet like the feet of a deer;
   he enables me to stand on the heights.
He trains my hands for battle;
   my arms can bend a bow of bronze.
You give me your shield of victory,
   and your right hand sustains me;
   you stoop down to make me great.

Psalm 18:32–35

The Lord holds victory in store for the upright,
   he is a shield to those whose walk is blameless,
for he guards the course of the just
   and protects the way of his faithful ones.

Proverbs 2:7–8

*Everyone born of God overcomes the world. This is the
victory that has overcome the world, even our faith.
Who is it that overcomes the world? Only he who
believes that Jesus is the Son of God.*

1 John 5:4–5

God's Words of Life on
VICTORY

Though we live in the world, we do not wage war as the world does. The weapons we fight with are not the weapons of the world. On the contrary, they have divine power to demolish strongholds. We demolish arguments and every pretension that sets itself up against the knowledge of God, and we take captive every thought to make it obedient to Christ.

2 Corinthians 10:3–5

Lift up your heads, O you gates;
    be lifted up, you ancient doors,
    that the King of glory may come in.
Who is this King of glory?
    The LORD strong and mighty,
    the LORD mighty in battle.

Psalm 24:7–8

To God belong strength and victory.

Job 12:16

We will shout for joy when you are victorious
    and will lift up our banners in the name of our God.

Psalm 20:5

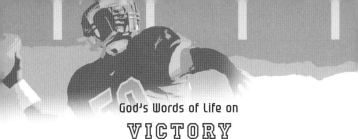

God's Words of Life on
VICTORY

The LORD is a warrior;
the LORD is his name.

Exodus 15:3

Shouts of joy and victory
resound in the tents of the righteous:
"The LORD's right hand has done mighty things!"

Psalm 118:15

Your right hand, O LORD,
was majestic in power.
Your right hand, O LORD,
shattered the enemy.

Exodus 15:6

I do not trust in my bow, O LORD,
my sword does not bring me victory;
but you give us victory over our enemies,
you put our adversaries to shame.
In God we make our boast all day long,
and we will praise your name forever.

Psalm 44:6–8

God's Words of Life on
VICTORY

It was not by their sword that they won the land,
 O LORD,
  nor did their arm bring them victory;
it was your right hand, your arm,
  and the light of your face, for you loved them.
Psalm 44:3

Do not be afraid. Stand firm and you will see the deliverance the LORD will bring you today.... The LORD will fight for you; you need only to be still.
Exodus 14:13–14

Jesus said, "In this world you will have trouble. But take heart! I have overcome the world."
John 16:33

Fight the good fight of the faith. Take hold of the eternal life to which you were called when you made your good confession in the presence of many witnesses.
1 Timothy 6:12

I can do everything through God who gives me strength.
Philippians 4:13

Thanks be to God! He gives us the victory through our Lord Jesus Christ.
1 Corinthians 15:57

God's Words of Life on

VICTORY

The LORD thundered from heaven;
 the voice of the Most High resounded.
He shot his arrows and scattered the enemies,
 great bolts of lightning and routed them.

Psalm 18:13–14

*Joshua, by then old and well advanced in years,
summoned all Israel—their elders, leaders, judges and
officials—and said to them: ... "You yourselves have
seen everything the LORD your God has done to all
these nations for your sake; it was the LORD your God
who fought for you. Remember how I have allotted as
an inheritance for your tribes all the land of the nations
that remain—the nations I conquered—between the
Jordan and the Great Sea in the west. The LORD your
God himself will drive them out of your way. He will
push them out before you, and you will take possession
of their land, as the LORD your God promised you. Be
very strong; be careful to obey all that is written in the
Book of the Law of Moses, without turning aside to the
right or to the left. Do not associate with these nations
that remain among you; do not invoke the names of
their gods or swear by them. You must not serve them
or bow down to them. But you are to hold fast to the
LORD your God, as you have until now. The LORD has
driven out before you great and powerful nations; to
this day no one has been able to withstand you. One of
you routs a thousand, because the LORD your God fights
for you, just as he promised. So be very careful to love
the LORD your God."*

Joshua 23:1–11

Devotional Thought on
VICTORY

Coach's pep talks are a part of sports lore. And no pep talks are more famous than those of the famed Gipper, George Gipp, of Notre Dame football. Down through the years, his legendary halftime speeches have influenced many coaches who wanted to crank up their players with pregame and halftime speeches.

In Joshua 23, we find that Joshua is now old. His days as the leader of the Israelites are numbered. His successes were many, but his future is short. So he gathers together the elders, leaders, judges, and officials and proceeds to give them a pep talk to end all pep talks. And he isn't talking about winning a football game—he's talking about winning God's battles.

Joshua wanted to leave the people with a clear understanding of the game plan for the future. Notice what he told them:

Look to God for the victory (verse 5).

Be strong (verse 6).

Follow the rules (verse 6).

Remain spiritually pure (verse 7).

Love God (verse 11).

"The Josher" set forth a game plan that we would do well to follow.

Imagine how our lives would change if we were to follow those five guidelines: trust God, be strong, obey God, remain pure, and love God.

That's a sure strategy for success in the Christian life.

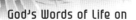

God's Words of Life on

WEAKER TEAMMATES

Be careful ... that the exercise of your freedom does not become a stumbling block to the weak.

1 Corinthians 8:9

Make up your mind not to put any stumbling block or obstacle in your brother's way. As one who is in the Lord Jesus, I am fully convinced that no food is unclean in itself. But if anyone regards something as unclean, then for him it is unclean. If your brother is distressed because of what you eat, you are no longer acting in love. Do not by your eating destroy your brother for whom Christ died. Do not allow what you consider good to be spoken of as evil. For the kingdom of God is not a matter of eating and drinking, but of righteousness, peace and joy in the Holy Spirit, because anyone who serves Christ in this way is pleasing to God and approved by men.

Romans 14:13–18

Jesus said, "What goes into a man's mouth does not make him 'unclean,' but what comes out of his mouth, that is what makes him 'unclean.'"

Matthew 15:11

Encourage the timid, help the weak, be patient with everyone.

1 Thessalonians 5:14

God's Words of Life on
WEAKER TEAMMATES

Do not destroy the work of God for the sake of food. All food is clean, but it is wrong for a man to eat anything that causes someone else to stumble. It is better not to eat meat or drink wine or to do anything else that will cause your brother to fall.

Romans 14:20–21

Strengthen your feeble arms and weak knees. "Make level paths for your feet," so that the lame may not be disabled, but rather healed.

Hebrews 12:12–13

Accept him whose faith is weak, without passing judgment on disputable matters. One man's faith allows him to eat everything, but another man, whose faith is weak, eats only vegetables. The man who eats everything must not look down on him who does not, and the man who does not eat everything must not condemn the man who does, for God has accepted him. Who are you to judge someone else's servant? To his own master he stands or falls. And he will stand, for the Lord is able to make him stand.

Romans 14:1–4

We who are strong ought to bear with the failings of the weak and not to please ourselves. Each of us should please his neighbor for his good, to build him up.

Romans 15:1–2

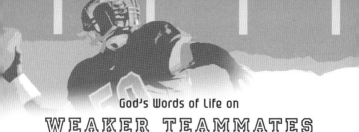

God's Words of Life on

WEAKER TEAMMATES

Do not cause anyone to stumble.

1 Corinthians 10:32

One man considers one day more sacred than another; another man considers every day alike. Each one should be fully convinced in his own mind. He who regards one day as special, does so to the Lord. He who eats meat, eats to the Lord, for he gives thanks to God; and he who abstains, does so to the Lord and gives thanks to God. For none of us lives to himself alone and none of us dies to himself alone. If we live, we live to the Lord; and if we die, we die to the Lord. So, whether we live or die, we belong to the Lord.

Romans 14:5–8

Food does not bring us near to God; we are no worse if we do not eat, and no better if we do.

1 Corinthians 8:8

If what I eat causes my brother to fall into sin, I will never eat [it] again, so that I will not cause him to fall.

1 Corinthians 8:13

We put no stumbling block in anyone's path.

2 Corinthians 6:3

Set an example for the believers in speech, in life, in love, in faith and in purity.

1 Timothy 4:12

Devotional Thought on
WEAKER TEAMMATES

Who is watching you? For most of us, our world of influence is not very big. Our families may be observing us, or perhaps our neighbors, some folks at church, or our co-workers are watching us.

But even in our small spheres of influence, we must remember that among those observing us will be some people whom Paul calls "the weak." These are folks who are younger or less mature in the faith, and we may easily influence them in a negative way.

It's similar to the care and feeding of infants. You have to be very careful to feed them foods that will build them up, not tear them down.

Think now about Christian athletes. They have huge spheres of influence, and they must take the "weaker brother or sister" concept seriously. Sometimes, though, I'm afraid they don't think too much about it.

Take one NFL quarterback, for instance. Although he has spoken out about his faith in Christ without fear, he also was reported in a national magazine article to have done some things that might cause younger Christians to stumble—things related to alcohol consumption and bad language.

Anyone who is in Christian leadership must recognize that each activity is an opportunity—either for building fellow believers up or for putting a stumbling block in their way.

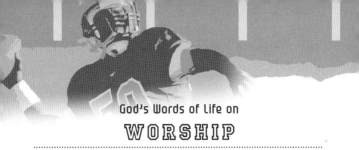

God's Words of Life on
WORSHIP

You are worthy, our Lord and God,
    to receive glory and honor and power,
for you created all things,
    and by your will they were created
    and have their being.

Revelation 4:11

Exalt the LORD our God
    and worship at his footstool;
    he is holy.

Psalm 99:5

Glory to God in the highest,
    and on earth peace to men on whom his favor rests.

Luke 2:14

Amen!
Praise and glory
and wisdom and thanks and honor
and power and strength
be to our God for ever and ever.
Amen!

Revelation 7:12

God's Words of Life on
WORSHIP

O LORD my God, you are very great;
  you are clothed with splendor and majesty.
He wraps himself in light as with a garment;
  he stretches out the heavens like a tent
  and lays the beams of his upper chambers on
    their waters.
He makes the clouds his chariot
  and rides on the wings of the wind.

Psalm 104:1–3

Be exalted, O God, above the heavens;
  let your glory be over all the earth.

Psalm 57:5

Holy, holy, holy
  is the Lord God Almighty,
  who was, and is, and is to come.

Revelation 4:8

Clap your hands, all you nations;
  shout to God with cries of joy.
How awesome is the LORD Most High,
  the great King over all the earth!

Psalm 47:1–2

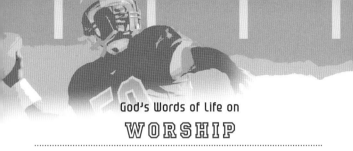

God's Words of Life on

WORSHIP

Ascribe to the LORD, O families of nations,
    ascribe to the LORD glory and strength,
    ascribe to the LORD the glory due his name.
Bring an offering and come before him;
    worship the LORD in the splendor of his holiness.

1 Chronicles 16:28–29

Let them praise the name of the LORD,
    for his name alone is exalted;
    his splendor is above the earth and the heavens.

Psalm 148:13

*I saw the Lord seated on a throne, high and exalted, and the
train of his robe filled the temple. Above him were seraphs,
each with six wings: With two wings they covered their
faces, with two they covered their feet, and with two they
were flying. And they were calling to one another:*

"Holy, holy, holy is the LORD Almighty;
    the whole earth is full of his glory."

Isaiah 6:1–3

Worthy is the Lamb, who was slain,
to receive power and wealth and wisdom and strength
and honor and glory and praise!...
To him who sits on the throne and to the Lamb
be praise and honor and glory and power,
    for ever and ever!

Revelation 5:12–13

God's Words of Life on
WORSHIP

The name of the LORD will be declared in Zion
    and his praise in Jerusalem
when the peoples and the kingdoms
    assemble to worship the LORD.

Psalm 102:21–22

Lift your eyes and look to the heavens:
    Who created all these?
He who brings out the starry host one by one,
    and calls them each by name.
Because of his great power and mighty strength,
    not one of them is missing.

Isaiah 40:26

The heavens praise your wonders, O LORD,
    your faithfulness too, in the assembly of the holy
        ones.
For who in the skies above can compare with the LORD?
    Who is like the LORD among the heavenly beings?
In the council of the holy ones God is greatly feared;
    he is more awesome than all who surround him.
O LORD God Almighty, who is like you?
    You are mighty, O LORD, and your faithfulness
        surrounds you.

Psalm 89:5–8

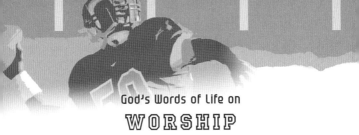

God's Words of Life on

WORSHIP

Shout for joy to the LORD, all the earth.
  Worship the LORD with gladness;
  come before him with joyful songs.
Know that the LORD is God.
  It is he who made us, and we are his.

Psalm 100:1–3

Lift up your heads, O you gates;
  lift them up, you ancient doors,
  that the King of glory may come in.
Who is he, this King of glory?
  The LORD Almighty—
  he is the King of glory.

Psalm 24:9–10

Come, let us bow down in worship,
  let us kneel before the LORD our Maker;
for he is our God
  and we are the people of his pasture,
  the flock under his care.

Psalm 95:6–7

Devotional Thought on
WORSHIP

Can an athlete worship God all the time? Can a fan? Is it too much to ask busy people with championships to win and families to raise and life to live to worship God all the time?

Former college football star and network football analyst Todd Blackledge doesn't think so. He realizes that, because of all God has done for us, there's not enough time to give God enough praise.

"God formed us and fashioned us and made us in a very unique way," said Blackledge. "I think one of the things he desired for his creation to do is to worship him. And to worship him, not on just a Sunday morning, not singing a song, or singing in the choir, but just in the way we live our lives. And how we live them, moment-to-moment, can be an expression of worship."

Athletes and non-athletes alike have the opportunity to glorify God in all we do. The psalmist called us the "people of [God's] pasture, the flock under his care" (Psalm 95:7), which means that we are totally dependent on God. That truth alone should remind us that we must praise God with every breath and in every action.

Today, begin to practice this truth. Worship God all the time, and watch what a difference it makes in your life.

At Inspirio we love to hear from you—
your stories, your feedback,
and your product ideas.
Please send your comments to us
by way of e-mail at
icares@zondervan.com
or to the address below:

inspirio

Attn: Inspirio Cares
5300 Patterson Avenue SE
Grand Rapids, MI 49530

If you would like further information
about Inspirio and the products we
create, please visit us at:
www.inspiriogifts.com

Thank you and God bless!

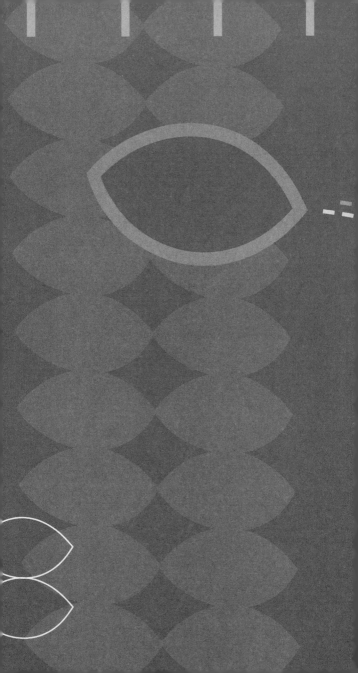